Contents

Zakes Mda

And the Girls in their Sunday Dresses

Four Works

ZAKES MDA

WUP Witwatersrand University Press

Witwatersrand University Press
1 Jan Smuts Avenue
Johannesburg
2001
South Africa

ISBN 13: 978 1 86814 222 4

First published in 1993
Second printing 2004
Third printing 2009
Fourth printing 2013
Typeset by Kohler Carton and Print (Natal)
Printed and bound by Creda Communications, Cape Town

Witwatersrand University Press acknowledges with thanks the contribution of Albio Gonzalez who was responsible for all the graphic illustrations used in this book.

Cover design by Sue Sandrock

And
the Girls in
their Sunday
Dresses

Introduction

Bhekizizwe Peterson

And the Girls in Their Sunday Dresses: Four Works marks an important achievement in South African theatre – the publication of a second collection of plays and a cinepoem script written by Zakes Mda. The first collection, *We Shall Sing for the Fatherland and Other Plays*, was brought out by Ravan Press in 1980 and subsequently expanded and reissued in 1990 under the new title *The Plays of Zakes Mda.*

Mda's unusual distinction, particularly for a black playwright, can be partially accounted for by his unique status and location in the history of South African theatre. It is the consequence of his peculiar biography, dramatic skills and the thematic concerns of his plays. Inasmuch as Mda's creative and theoretical works are part of the black theatre movement which crystallised in the seventies, there is no mistaking the many ways in which his work goes against the grain of the performance traditions and politics of the same movement.

Zanemvula Kizito Gatyeni Mda was born on 6 October 1948 in Sterkspruit, Herschel District, in the eastern Cape Province. He was the first child of three boys and one girl born to Ashby Peter Solomzi and Rose Nompumelelo Mda. Soon after his birth the Mda family moved to Johannesburg and Zanemvula grew up in Orlando East and, later on, in Dobsonville, Soweto.

He returned to Herschel in his teens, initially to visit his grandparents during school holidays and later when his parents, trying to isolate him from mischief in Soweto, decided that he should attend school in Herschel. Mda was joined by his father who returned to Sterkspruit to practise as a lawyer. His recollections of the Herschel district are anchored in its desolate landscape and the stark poverty that characterised most peasant households.

Mda's year of birth also marked the accession to parliamentary control of South African politics and society of the National Party – a political development that was to be of great import to the Mda family. In the fifties the National Party government embarked on a consistent campaign to enforce racial segregation and to eradicate radical African opposition to its policies, especially that initiated by the African National Congress and the Pan Africanist Congress.

Mda senior was a key and vocal opponent of apartheid, initially as a founder member and important theoretician of the African National Congress's Youth League, formed in 1943, and later as a founder member of the Pan Africanist Congress. The early sixties saw Mda senior arrested for his political activities. In 1963, after securing bail, he left South Africa for Lesotho where he went into political exile. The rest of the family followed within a year.

Consequently, Zakes Mda received all his high school education in Lesotho. He studied law for a while after matriculating but then decided to change direction, pursuing instead a course in the arts and humanities.

Mda's first forays into creative work were in the visual arts – primarily painting. It was only later that he started writing plays. He had been exposed to theatre, and especially to the work of Gibson Kente, in South Africa. He recalls the first play that he saw as being a performance of Kente's *Manana the Jazz Prophet* in Sterkspruit. Kente continued to exercise an influence on Mda even in Lesotho where Mda saw another of his productions – *Sikhalo*.

Mda's first attempts at writing plays were in the late sixties while he was still at high school when he produced works very much in the mould of Kenteesque musicals. Though he appreciated the popular aesthetics and appeal of Kente, especially as imbedded in his use of music and dance, Mda was less sure about the dramatic and political cogency of Kente's plays. The shift away from Kente came as Mda was exposed, through his personal reading and abiding interest in political and cultural affairs, to the works of African and international playwrights.

Another South African playwright who was to exercise a considerable influence on Mda was Dukuza ka Macu who spent about five years in Lesotho from the late seventies. ka Macu's major works are *The Blackman's Kingdom*, *Heaven Weep for Thina Sonke* and *Night of the Long Wake* and his uncelebrated status is a telling reminder of the inequalities that persist in South African theatre and publishing.

The key thematic affinities that can be observed in the works of Mda and ka Macu is their empathy with the experiences of common people and their profound appreciation of the possibilities contained in the foregrounding of the black family as the locus of dramatic action.

In the eighties black theatre, with the exception of township melodramas, tended to shy away from exploring familial conflicts as a catalyst for delineating broader social and political patterns. The preferred locations were the streets, schools, prisons, rallies and other public spaces where the protagonists tended to derive their identities largely, if not solely, from their involvement in the political struggle. Mda and ka Macu's ability to see the connections between the personal and the public, especially as evidenced in the social affliction and fragmentation that threatens the black family, makes their works accessible to African audiences because they reflect so many of their lives.

Stylistically, the theatrical experimentation of both playwrights is often tempered by elegant writing and a keen sense of dialogue.

The settings of Mda's plays are stark, like the socio-political environment in which his characters find themselves. The action of the plays is frequently located in a number of acting areas, mostly three platforms of varying levels. The different levels and performance spaces acquire various symbolic and dramatic meanings during the unfolding of the narrative. The spaces can represent the social and power hierarchies operative in the society or they can chart the physicality of the quest upon which the characters embark – what Mda refers to as the 'different periods in the history of our characters'. (A note with exactly this wording appears in two of Mda's plays – *Joys of War* and *The Nun*.)

Consistent with their underclass status in a colonial or neo-colonial society in which they are denied political and economic rights, Mda's characters enter the barren Southern African landscape with little except their own sense of dignity and survival. We rarely meet them in their homes; instead we constantly find them adrift on personal and historical journeys. (*Banned* is the exception in this collection.) They are either on the road or waiting at some impersonal social or governmental space. The thread of being caught between two worlds – oppression and liberation, the roads leading away from home towards the capital and its spaces of petty officialdom – obviously parallels the distances covered by the Mda family and their own sense of marking time.

What redeems the desolation is the unyielding struggle of the characters to secure the means of life and to have their human status recognised. The possibilities of life and growth that we encounter in the dramas, then, are located in the characters themselves and not elsewhere. The characterisation hovers between individuality and typicality. At the beginning of the narratives the characters are introduced as types – characters who embody the typical historical and social contradictions of their time and space: Mama, Nana, soldiers and so on. It is only when they start to twist and turn under the weight of the historical exigencies that confront them that we encounter them anew as specific individuals living out a general incongruity.

Apart from the thematic richness presented to us by Mda's stark settings, their other importance lies in how, in acting terms, they focus the energies of the actors on the significance of performance itself. It is left to the performers to sketch in the details of space and environment, time and atmosphere. There are no short cuts through the use of elaborate sets or technical wizardry. Like the characters they portray, the actors are expected to journey with very little else but the dramatic skills that they possess. The success of Mda's theatre, whether on the level of theme, performance or organisation, relies on human resources.

In terms of the politics of organising theatre as a social activity Mda's plays are portable; they can be performed anywhere without losing their essence because of the absence of the standard paraphernalia of the theatre.

In order to understand the thematic preoccupations of Mda one has to appreciate the special influences that were brought to bear on his thinking by his exile in Lesotho. There his ideology was shaped by two powerful currents. Firstly, he retained a keen interest in the nationalist politics of the liberation movements and followed with fascination the political and cultural efficacy of the Black Consciousness Movement in the seventies and eighties. The imperatives of South African nationalism brought to the fore the need to explore the themes of racism and oppression, migrancy and its impact on the family structure and the attendant politics of gender, and resistance strategies ranging from personal confrontations of the system to the socio-political intentions of armed insurrection. Whatever the particular focus foregrounded in his dramas, the plays, consistent with the tenor of much black theatre, are intent on restoring individual and cultural integrity and self-worth and on explaining and inspiring the need for active resistance.

At the same time, as strong as such nationalist concerns are in the texts, they are generally subtly qualified, if not outrightly called into question, by the second stream of influence on Mda – his proximity to the crystallising neo-colonial dependency of Lesotho on South Africa. So we see in the plays, below the sharp calls for nationalist resistance, muted rumblings about the dangers of neo-colonialism.

In this collection, this difficult dialogue can be observed in *Banned*, *Joys of War* and in *And The Girls in their Sunday Dresses.*

Banned is a radio play adapted by Mda from a film script, *Smouldering*, in 1982. *Banned* strikes me as a hesitant exploration of the nationalist themes that Mda was to develop more successfully in *Joys of War*. The recurring motifs are the plight of homeless people, the social and other violence that emanates from the state, the futility of peaceful protests and the need to accept the necessity of sacrifice if more militant forms such as the armed struggle are to be embarked upon. Both plays use squatter camps as important dramatic frames, with the shacks being razed and rebuilt with a regularity that is meant to emphasise resilience.

Banned is set in Alexandra township and starts off with a depiction of the absurdities of South African law as it is evinced in the life experiences of the two protagonists. The play, in essence, traces the political growth of Cynthia, a social worker who becomes disenchanted with her profession, and Bra Zet, a paralysed gangster who, initially, is merely content with keeping alive the popular legends of his previous notoriety.

The two characters are catapulted into a relationship when Cynthia, against her wishes, is assigned to counsel Bra Zet. The relationship develops from mutual distrust to a discovery of the humanity in each other and, amidst the increasing political opposition in the township, that of other township dwellers despite the alienation and squalor to which they are fettered. The scene is then set for the violent encounter between the community and the state. The confrontation is in many ways merely an antecedent to the implied major conflict that is still to come, that of armed insurrection.

Banned uses a dynamic manipulation of time, fusing past and present into an evocative suggestion of the potency of experience and memory as political weapons. And yet it is arguably the motif of memory that fails to work as a dramatic catalyst. This is because it shifts the focus away from character motivations and interactions, leaning more towards charting the steps that lead to the banning of Cynthia and the murder of Bra Zet by the police. Some of the scenes come across as illustrative enactments rather than as dramatic moments which extend the exploration of conflict and characterisation. Consequently, characterisation is at best two dimensional and the possibilities of achieving more with less, with regard to content and form, were to be realised only in *Joys of War*.

The writing of *Joys of War* was inspired by a visit by Mda to Central America. During his travels and participation in theatre for development workshops, Mda met an old woman in a village who recounted her travels from city to city looking for her son. The similarity between this story and many other families' experiences in Southern Africa, especially after the large scale move into exile by activists after the 1976 uprising, meant that it could be located and extended in a South African context.

The quest motif remains a thematic constant (developed in a number of significant ways) and is also embedded in the dramatic structure of the play. The action of *Joys of War* takes place on three levels and shifts subtly between them in a manner that reveals the continuities between the different levels and character experiences. This is achieved mainly through the use of two dramatic techniques.

Firstly, there are moments when the characters on the different levels seemingly pick up on each other's dialogue but with slight variations in emphasis. We can observe this technique in the discussions on the death of babies, (p 91), interrogation chambers (p 110) and the events preceding Soldier One's flight into exile (pp 115–16). There are also moments when characters on one level are able to observe, like the audience, the experiences of the others (p 109).

At the start of the play we find two soldiers in silhouette, on the highest level, reminiscent of statues in a war memorial. The level on which the soldiers are located, we learn at the end, is the thematic icon that anchors the drama. It signifies the quest for commitment and sacrifice, the supreme level of activism that the struggle for liberation demands. The life experiences of the two soldiers are outlined through their recollections and interactions. They have been thrown together because of the exigencies of the armed struggle and their encounters allow us an entrée into their personal vulnerabilities and different motivations for joining the resistance movement.

Complementing the soldiers' process of self-discovery and increased commitment is the journey of Mama and Nana in search of Soldier One who, we are to discover, is the son of Mama and father to Nana.

It is through the experiences of Mama and Nana that we discern the social and political contexts that inform the actions of the soldiers. Soldier One comes from a squatter community whose endless battles with government officials committed to razing their shacks to the ground is captured in the myth of the phoenix that rises from the ashes.

The alienating and death-producing nature of apartheid is forcefully suggested in Nana's obsession with the well-being of her dolls – a concern with the condition of children which is common in the populace (p 103). Her infatuation signifies the constancy of death in the African community because of the racism and socio-political violence that are the consequences of apartheid and the uneven development of the country. Social resources and amenities are concentrated in the cities and access is denied to the poor and labouring classes (pp 89, 103). Nana's preoccupation with her dolls also encapsulates her struggle to retain her youthful status in the face of social pressures to assume adult responsibilities – a futile exercise as far as Mama is concerned as she was 'born a young woman' (p 87).

Unlike the phoenix in the myth which sets itself alight on a funeral pyre only to rise again to relive life with new youth and vigour ('. . . young with beautiful red and gold feathers' – p 88), it is the government officials who set the squatters' households and belongings on fire. The squatters, in a search analogous to the phoenix's quest for life and beauty, stop their intermittent wanderings and '. . . rebuild from the ashes' (p 88), patiently waiting for the day when the national colours of the liberation movements (black, gold and green) will replace the austerity and aridness of the ashes (p 88).

In preparation for such an event the squatters engage in campaigns against the authorities. Soldier One once played a leading role in these campaigns and his sudden and unexplained departure throws the community into turmoil as it smacks of betrayal. The need to refute the increasing rumours and to ascertain the reasons for his departure is what sets Mama and Nana on the road looking for him. Mama is under the impression that he is in detention. Soldier One's departure is motivated by his realisation that 'we can't just go on rebuilding . . . We got to do something to stop the destruction permanently' (p 96).

In the two soldiers we have the complex and, at times, conflicting reasons that inform peoples' decisions to commit themselves to political activism. They are generally opposites in terms of the shading of their characters (extrovert vs introvert) and this sets up an intriguing interest in locating the different motives that drive their actions. From their common awareness of the suffering that governs the lives of blacks they tease out dissimilar appreciations of black people's resilience and their forms of resistance.

For instance when reflecting on the seemingly eternal presence of funerals in the black community, Soldier Two prefers to remember them as symbolic of the stubborn humanity and resilience of oppressed communities; their ability to retain their compassion and frailties even under the most macabre of circumstances, such as wakes being transformed into social occasions (p 97). Soldier One, on the other hand, experiences funerals as militant spectacles in which freedom songs and clenched fists sculpture the anger and militancy of the community (pp 98, 100).

Mda's primary focus, then, is on the profound psychic and social interiors that underlie the soldiers' surface behaviour. Because of the tension between a character's individuality and the social roles and demands imposed upon him or her, role-playing or 'acting', in its pejorative sense, is a strategy that is frequently utilised. This leads to the seemingly deceptive nature of human behaviour where Africans can assume identities that belie their real characters and thoughts (p 106). It is also of great moral import to people trying to rationalise the differences between general violence and the brutalities of war (p 111). An example of this is Soldier Two's approach to the war as a 'festival of fireworks' and a 'game' of 'draughts' (pp 122, 23).

Soldier One is the light-hearted and talkative one while Soldier Two is a reticent one-time poet who is now noted amongst his peers for his military daring and successes. It is in deconstructing the aura that surrounds Soldier Two's heroic status that we are made to confront the noble and ignoble tragedies and attendant ironies that make up the joys of war.

The play is rich with thematic metaphors in this regard. One can elucidate extensively on the connotations between Soldier One's insistent chattering and his search for truth and freedom and Soldier Two's courage and reticence and the guilt-informed psychic repressions that he experiences. Yet there is a sense in which Mda undercuts the crises and paradoxes that run profoundly through the joys of nationalist wars throughout the continent. Although the need for armed insurrection is incontestable given the specific colonial predicaments faced by Africans, there is a thin line between accepting that reality – 'from Bullets flowers shall bloom' (p 100) – and slowly sliding into militarist celebrations of the 'redemptive powers' of violence or the 'armed struggle'.

The supposition that we can '. . . cleanse our souls with violence' – as also argued in Mda's *The Road* – had, and still has a lot of currency in opposition circles. In the seventies it stemmed largely from an awareness of the real political and social gains that liberation movements such as Frelimo and the MPLA were able to achieve through armed resistance despite the intransigence of the colonial forces. But such deifications of armed resistance bring forth at least two other difficulties: firstly, a tendency to undervalue, consciously or unconsciously, other forms of resistance, and, secondly, a turning away from exploring the paradoxes of violence.

It is of course simplistic to try and assign different levels of significance to different forms of resistance based on the assumed personal and moral claims that each makes. In this regard the 'armed struggle' cannot be elevated in importance above the various forms of struggle that are embarked upon in the sphere of civil society. Mda's sensitivity to the daily toils of families, peasants and labourers is an important check on such assumptions. And yet in *Joys of War* (and also in an earlier play, *Dark Voices Ring*) Mda seems, ultimately, to privilege armed insurrection despite its ambiguities and interconnections with other forms of resistance.

This friction is apparent in Mda's denial, in a note to me, that he creates any hierarchy between types of resistance. His explanation does, however, indicate the implicit tensions when he explains the turn to armed resistance in the following terms: 'In the seventies some of us saw no other option, and at every available opportunity we wanted to drum it home to the people that all else has failed, and that the armed struggle was justified.'

In *Joys of War* we can detect this in the play's insistence on retracing the steps only of the soldiers' growth and the fact that Nana's main significance lies not in her past experiences but in the future tasks she will perform as a soldier.

The soldiers' understanding of the need for armed insurrection is what identifies them as unique activists and distinguishes them from the mass that enters and exits the stage only to confirm the appropriateness of the soldiers' designation. Hence, for most of the play the soldiers are located on the top plane of the stage in what I take to be Mda's largely unstated moral accreditation of the various forms of resistance.

It is when the wretched reasons that underlie Soldier Two's commitment are disclosed that the moral distance between the levels is destroyed and we are told that 'from now on all the levels shall belong to the same space and time' (p 138). The action then takes place on the intermediary second level during the following moments of indecision in the play.

The spatial and moral order is re-established at the end of the play by two developments. Firstly Soldier Two achieves personal and political atonement by committing suicide, thereby freeing Soldier One and the audience of the dilemma of working out the appropriate penalty. The suicide is also an unconvincing attempt by Mda to imbue his death and the attendant unresolved struggle with dignity and hope, for Soldier Two's decision to kill himself is prompted by Nana's statement that she too wants to be a soldier (p 143). His death therefore serves, more significantly, as a rite of passage for Nana's growth from her child-like status and make-believe world of dolls to her assumption of the role of Soldier Two in the mission. Her transformation suggests the desired progression in commitment and it is clearly meant to override her previous status, whatever the social critiques enshrined in her signification during her early stage (p 145).

Far from creating the 'new man and woman', as numerous simplifications of Fanon's thesis on violence suggest, the participation in armed insurrection has no straightforward redemptive benefits for the individuals or communities concerned, especially on the level of ideology. The implications of violence and war for the psychological make-up of individuals – a significant number of whom are children in the Southern African context – is of course deeply complicated. *Joys of War* is a bold attempt at delineating such consequences but its insights are in places limited by the romantic nationalism that governs its narrative assumptions.

In *And the Girls in their Sunday Dresses* Mda turns his attention to the problems of dependency in Lesotho and, in the process, subtly calls into question a number of nationalist assumptions. The plot is deceptively simple but around it are woven a range of complicated themes. The narrative action centres on the efforts of two women to buy rice at a government food aid depot. We encounter them three or four days after their arrival, still waiting, and we gradually get to hear their personal testimonies. While the play is set in Lesotho, it gestures constantly towards Lesotho's socio-economic dependency on South Africa. One of Mda's main arguments is that the relationship between the two countries should not be lost sight of and their political struggles and socio-economic contradictions should be tackled from the perspective of the entire Southern African region (p 26).

The two characters, simply called The Lady and The Woman, start off as broad social types representing the relatively different experiences of city/educated and rural/unskilled women. Despite his apparent empathy for both characters, Mda's descriptions clearly establish The Woman as the one who is to enjoy authorial approval throughout the drama; the playwright in his stage directions extols her sober and motherly appearance in comparison to the 'pretentious' and 'sexy' nature of The Lady (p 4). However, there are a lot of common experiences between these contrasting identities that are predicated on the politics of gender and the social roles that women are expected to perform in society ('we are all victims of a social order . . .' – p 20). Both women have lost faith in the possibility of any meaningful relationship with men. It emerges that they have both been involved with the same man – an Italian – and in each case the outcome was the same: desertion. As The Lady so eloquently universalises their experience, 'men . . . they are the same. They are like children of one person' (p 37).

The preference for European males reflects at least three related determinants: a feeling of self-hatred, the generally abusive and exploitative nature of relationships with men of whatever nationality (with 'local men' being presumably 'even worse' – p 20) and the perception of white men as possible avenues of escape from the poverty of Southern Africa.

Saturated with the prevalent social definition of beauty and whiteness as synonymous, the women in their youth tried to deface their blackness with skin lightening creams (p 8). This racism is compatible with sexism – the need to 'look beautiful for . . . other people' (p 9), the hope that marriage can serve as some form of insurance policy (p 21) and the general expectation that to ensure employment and promotion women have to consent to the sexual advances of their male colleagues (p 19). If all else fails, the preferred solution is to marry European men who, it is felt, can facilitate 'respectable lives as housewives' (p 21).

Caught between such pressures, the women either regain their self-worth and dignity – as in the case of The Woman – or slide further into self-destructive responses like prostitution – as typified by The Lady. The Lady deludes herself that she is able to avenge herself through her activities as a prostitute (p 20). Her short-sightedness, and that of women who find solace in religion, is questioned by The Woman who prefers instead to emphasise social resolutions that link the subordination of women with broader political and economic contradictions. As she observes at one point, 'Is it not through politics that the laws that have created these terrible conditions for us are made?' (p 26).

Appropriate responses foregrounded by The Woman include labour organisation, fighting against political apathy and nationalist nostalgia about the past, and promoting regional and collective strategies (p 26).

It is glaringly obvious, however, that all the responses high-lighted are more pertinent to the contestation of neo-colonial politics in Lesotho and not gender contradictions specifically. And in this lies both the play's strength and its weakness.

In *And the Girls in their Sunday Dresses* Mda, through a brilliantly understated derision of the new rulers and élites, shows how the gains of independence are denied the general populace by a self-satisfied, inefficient and corrupt bureaucracy. The depth of exploitation in the society is such that food donated by Western governments as aid to the poor – in itself nothing more than a re-creation of their cycle of poverty – is either sold by the government or made available to business for purchase and further merchandising.

The lower classes are acutely aware of these contradictions but they are content to adopt a wait-and-see attitude, sitting on 'the chair of patience' (p 37), and to offer whatever supplications and bribery are necessary to ensure their survival. It is this political inertia that The Woman feels must be abandoned for more active and radical forms of resistance. It is through analyses such as these and those contained in earlier plays – *We Shall Sing for the Fatherland* and *The Hill* for instance – that Mda warns about the ambiguities of African nationalism; that the expansive pan-class coalitions formed during the struggle against colonialism (and by inference against apartheid?) are likely to fracture in the post-apartheid period into, at least, the standard manifestations of class struggles.

As far as the imperatives of gender conflict are concerned, Mda falters after his initial substantial identification of the problem. His shortcoming is a common one in African performance where women, increasingly, are cast as protagonists who are broadly representative of a diverse range of marginalised and exploited social groups. Such typifications allow for insight into the experiences of the lower classes, of which women form a significant proportion, but they rarely highlight the specific predicaments that face women as a 'gendered' constituency. What tends to happen instead is that the contradictions that bedevil women's lives are approached as being just more manifestations of what is already identified as the primary contradiction, be it colonialism or neo-colonialism.

An indication of the subtle shifts, especially in terms of problem identification and resolution, that occur when the subordination of women is collapsed into common political oppression can be noted in the following extract in which The Woman's critique of male attitudes obliquely by-passes the issues of gender:

> It is now time for us to change things. To liberate not only ourselves, but the men themselves, for we are all in bondage! Yes, the men in this free and independent country are in bondage, mostly to their attitudes. That is why you see them sitting back and swimming in the glories of the past . . . We do not see much of what they are doing for the future. It is as if the past will take care of the future without any effort from the present. (p 27)

And the Girls in their Sunday Dresses would seem, therefore, to predicate the amelioration of women's subordination on the general political democratisation of society. History and feminists have demonstrated persuasively that democratisation of political institutions, whatever real gains it has for women as a social group, is more likely to lead to the re-configuration of gender subordination than its eradication.

The Final Dance is a striking confirmation of Mda's wide-ranging interests and audacious sense of experimentation. The cinepoem, as Mda aptly describes it, is a powerful contemplation on the age-old themes of social discrimination and the need for a humanism that overrides the short-sighted differentiations that we impose on our relations with 'others'. The focus is on two characters – an Old Man and a Little Girl – who overcome the class and age differences that should otherwise separate them. Their oneness is metaphorically captured in a waltz that they dance together. The familiarity of the theme is overcome by the fresh manner in which Mda retells the story.

The narrative operates very much like a poetic dance. The cinematic focus, in terms of camera angles, is constantly shifting from wide-angle shots to close-ups of subjects, locations and attendant detail. The feeling of movement in the piece is further sustained by the flexible use of time, garments and music. The Victorian character of the girl's family – with all its inevitable snobbishness and rigidity – is woven effortlessly into the contemporary 1990s life-style and poverty of the Old Man.

Whether Mda is gesturing towards distinct historical periods or rather, as I suspect, towards states of actuality and consciousness – opulence/European and poverty/'Third World?' – is largely inconsequential.

The strength of the narrative is precisely its constant questioning of the 'neat' categories or suppositions people create in their attempts to regulate their interactions with individuals from other class, racial, age or gender groups. For instance, how can we establish the identity of the protagonists? Does the Old Man's poverty within the Southern African context suggest that he is African and the Little Girl white? Then what do we make of his penchant for improvising a clownish dance to Kabalevsky's 'Comedians' Gallop'? Or of the fact that their moment of reconciliation and celebration is an appropriation of the waltz to Strauss's 'Tales from the Vienna Woods' that we initially associate with her haughty parents?

Even the end of the piece is the quintessence of ambiguity: the last image of the cinepoem is of the crowd, after watching the old man dance at the little girl's grave site, applauding 'albeit with placid, almost stone, cold faces. They applaud for a long long time.' (p 47)

For Mda it is enough that he has clearly stated the choices and actions that characters have to make in the betterment of their human and social condition. What actually happens thereafter is a matter to be resolved by his audience.

The open-ended conclusion of *The Final Dance* is, then, just another restatement of the profound, versatile nature of Mda's character and creativity. His adeptness in effortlessly switching to or mixing different art media is matched by the complex range of themes that occupy centre stage in his dramas.

The plays of Zakes Mda are impressive registers of the turbulent history of Southern Africa. What sets them apart from other theatrical accounts is Mda's rare acumen for distilling from the absurdities and grotesque experiences of apartheid Southern Africa credible characters whose profound humanity, pathos and resilience shine, whatever the odds stacked against them. Where many African playwrights in South Africa have, since the mid-seventies, preferred to address themselves to the more commercially viable task of cleansing 'liberal guilt' through replicating stereotypes and superficial critiques of conflict, Mda has settled for committed writing that is experimental and strikingly multifarious in its theatricality.

Zakes Mda: A Director's View

Teresa Devant

The first time I met somebody who knew about Zakes Mda's work was in Botswana in 1982 when I was head of the Theatre Unit of Medu Art Ensemble – a cultural group with a strong political agenda which was founded in Botswana by South African exiles in 1978 and ceased its activities after the South African Defence Force raid on Gaborone in June 1985.

At the time I was directing a play written and produced by the Ensemble. One of two South African actors who had been brought from Johannesburg to perform the play introduced me to Mda's activities as a dramatist. His comments were enthusiastic and I subsequently tried to follow up Mda's work.

Until then, my only knowledge of the work was through reviews of *We Shall Sing for the Fatherland*, a daring look at a post-revolutionary sitution after independence in an un-identified country. The message is universal but particularly relevant in the Southern African context.

I arrived in Maseru in 1986 by which time Mda was Senior Lecturer in the English Department at the National University of Lesotho in Roma and was well established as one of the most important playwrights in Southern Africa.

In Maseru, I founded Meso (Sesotho for 'dawn') Theatre Group together with a group of Basotho. To begin with, this ensemble performed poetry and drama with a well-defined working line on social and political issues which attracted Mda's interest. Years of professional co-operation followed and at the end of my stay in Lesotho I was asked to assist the University's English Department (of which Mda became head in 1991) for a year, holding weekly workshops in dramatic skills training.

In Maseru, a city with only about 100 000 inhabitants, it was easy to meet and communicate and I developed both a professional and a personal relationship with Zakes Mda based on contact between our families and his knowledge of my previous work with South African playwrights, writers and artists during the lifetime of Medu Art Ensemble.

I am attracted to his frankness, his warm personality and his sense of humour as well as his inquisitiveness and interest in people, art and the environment.

A particular incident comes to my mind when I try to define his personality. While I was teaching at Roma University there was a student protest during which the army closed the university and students were barred from the campus. I telephoned Mda to tell him what was happening. His response was to drive immediately to Roma and help his students out of trouble.

In 1987 Mda came to my home one afternoon and gave me two manuscripts to read and comment upon. They were *Dankie Auntie*, a play for a relatively large cast, and a two-hander *And the Girls in their Sunday Dresses*. He offered to let me direct the latter. The manuscript gave me a new insight into Mda's work. I was captivated by the scintillating quality of the dialogue in which endemic social traumas were treated with piercing satire. I found in the play the Brechtian vein which is one of the strengths of Mda's work.

And the Girls in their Sunday Dresses which was originally performed at the 1988 Edinburgh Fringe Festival was the first play representing Lesotho to be performed abroad and was well received by the critics. The two actresses cast in its demanding roles had never had formal training or performed before – one was a journalist, the other a pharmacist.

It is rare for a playwright and a director to sustain a lasting working relationship as they often live apart geographically and do not always understand a work in the same way. In the case of Mda and myself, neither of those factors affected our relationship.

Mda's involvement in the production of his plays is limited to a minimum – a fact he makes clear from the start. He acts as a distant observer, giving full responsibility to the director and great freedom during rehearsals. This trust in respect of substance and artistic matters has resulted in the establishment of a very strong bond between us.

Although he is reluctant to see his own plays on the stage, he is extremely interested in the response of the audience to the final form of the director's perception and interpretation of his work.

Zakes Mda's creative power ranges from writing to composing music, producing films and video programmes and painting. He strives to achieve great accuracy in the details of the surroundings in which his works are set and studies these at length and, when necessary, on location.

His dramatic work differs from that of his contemporary colleagues in that he distances himself from a theatre of art-for-art's sake in which social analysis comes second to entertainment and which uses proven elements of hilarity such as funerals, weddings, street scenes, drunkards and so on to entertain. This approach puts the emphasis on the wrong element – entertainment values deriving from the tragic quotidian life of black communities – without delving into a deeper cause and effect analysis of that situation. Playwrights following this line plead for reform through a theatre of acceptance and complaint.

But neither does his dramatic production fall within the scope and approach of playwrights who address their works largely at white urban audiences and express protest by depicting the hopelessness of the situation of the oppressed without analysing the past or scrutinising the future.

Mda's works, particularly those produced in the last fifteen years, form a theatre of resistance which aims to conscientise and mobilise the oppressed. In them we find a scrutiny of the society in which Mda's criticism brings out the contradictions, the aspirations and the frustrations of the oppressed. Motivation for the struggle for liberation; traditional versus modern social values; corruption, exploitation and gender issues become central to the analysis.

His use, as in *Joys of War*, of cinematographic methods in which the story unfolds through two simultaneous passages in which the action breaks all dimensional bounds in terms of space and time without losing the unity of the narrative is akin to the technique in Velazquez's masterpiece *Las Meninas* in which the painter depicts the same scene from two different angles by means of a mirror. It is a method which has not been used up to now in African theatre.

Role-playing, together with the time-space elements are the major constants in Mda's most recent dramatic works. His scenic vision may be influenced by Mda the visual art practitioner. The presence of symbolic elements in both the form and content of some of his latest plays brings him closer to expressionist theatre, distinguishing his work from the dramaturgy of many naturalist playwrights in Europe and Africa.

Zakes Mda's contribution to contemporary South African theatre is unique, personal and enriching. He succeeds in entertaining the audience without trivialising his material and in evoking a strong and generally positive response to the future. His open mindedness, his poignant social and political analysis and his search for new ways of handling a story using lights and interwoven space and time, put him in the forefront of South African dramatists.

And the Girls in their Sunday Dresses

AND THE GIRLS IN

THEIR SUNDAY

DRESSES

A Play

Characters

THE LADY

THE WOMAN

And the Girls in their Sunday Dresses was first performed during the Edinburgh Fringe Festival at Springwell House, Edinburgh, Scotland on 14 August 1988 by Meso Theatre Group. The Woman was played by Tokoloho Khutsoane and The Lady by Gertrude Mothibe. The production was directed by Teresa Devant. On 23 August the play opened at the West Indian Centre, Leeds with the same cast.

Scene 1

THE LADY *is about forty and a bit overdressed, albeit in the latest fashion. One can see that there was a conscious effort on her part to make herself appear very chic and sexy. Her mannerisms are of a sophisticated woman of the world, but of course at the end of it all she appears pretentious – even ridiculous. When the lights rise she is sitting on a chair, making herself up. She is looking at herself in a compact mirror and dabs a little powder on her cheeks. On her lap is all the paraphernalia used in make-up; lipstick, eyebrow pencils and mascara. She uses some more lipstick on her lips and tries to shape them in what she thinks is a sensuous way. Her old lizard bag lies opened on the ground.* THE WOMAN *enters holding a small parcel of food. She is much more simply and soberly dressed. Indeed she looks like someone's mother. She is roughly of the same age as* THE LADY.*

WOMAN: The queue hasn't moved an inch since I left.

LADY [*busy with her nails*]: Did you come with our lunch?

WOMAN [*throws packet to* THE LADY]: Here. Can't afford much more that that. Moreso we don't know for how long we'll be here.

Catches the packet, then puts her make-up paraphernalia into her handbag. She opens the packet and wolfs the food. Almost half-way through she remembers THE WOMAN.

4

LADY: Did you eat?

WOMAN: You know very well I did not eat.

LADY: I'll leave you some.

WOMAN: I'll eat it when I am on the chair.

THE LADY *has finished eating her share, and she gives what remains to* THE WOMAN. *Pause.*

LADY: It is the third day now.

WOMAN: Fourth.

LADY: Third.

WOMAN: For me it is the fourth.

LADY: And you managed without the chair. The first day, I mean. Before I came.

WOMAN: It had not rained then. I sat on the ground.

LADY: Yeah. It's wet all over now, so you need my chair. We need each other because I also need the food that you buy for both of us. You see, I didn't bring any money with me, and . . .

WOMAN: You told me already.

LADY: I just want you to understand that hands clean each other. You need my chair, I need your food. I don't want you to think I am stranded or something.

WOMAN: Maybe we should go.

LADY: Go? We wait here for days, then just when things are about to get right we go. Very clever.

WOMAN: How do you know things are about to get right? See, they are about to close and go for lunch.

LADY: They'll come back.

WOMAN: They always do. But we continue to wait.

LADY: Yeah.

WOMAN: So how do you know things are about to get right?

5

LADY: Dammit man, is it my fault that we have to wait here?

WOMAN: Nobody said it is.

LADY: Then stop bugging me, okay?

WOMAN [*coolly*]: We can all lose our temper if we want to, you know. We've all got it somewhere, and we can just as easily lose it.

[*There is the sound of a gong.*]

Ah, they are closing for lunch now.

LADY: I am sure when they come back things will be all right.

WOMAN: They are filing out of the storeroom.

LADY: And out of the offices.

WOMAN: Don't the office girls look beautiful in their summer dresses?

LADY [*contemptuously*]: Well, to you I am sure they do.

THE LADY *stands up, and they both wave at the throngs of people who are passing by.*

WOMAN: Goodbye, *marena-a-rona!*

LADY: Have a beautiful lunch.

WOMAN: As you chew think of us who are sitting here in the hot sun, and in the rain!

LADY [*to* THE WOMAN]: Why did you say that? Are you protesting or what? Do you want them to keep us here much longer than we have been? [*To the throngs*] She didn't mean it *bo-ntate le bo-'me'.* What she was trying to say is . . .

WOMAN: Who told you to speak on my behalf? I know exactly what I am trying to say. [*To the throngs*] What I am trying to say is, for how long do you think we'll wait here?

LADY: You see they are laughing at us. You want to make us a laughing stock of the storemen and office girls.

WOMAN: Listen! That other man answers. He says they are still sewing the bags. There is nothing they can do until all the bags have been sewn.

LADY: Of course they did tell us that right from scratch, didn't they? People have been buying a lot of this rice, they said. So it got finished in these storerooms, they said. They had to send trucks to fetch more rice from other hoarding places throughout the country. Now they are putting it into bags and sewing the bags. Some bags are tattered so they've got to be sewn before grain can be put into them.

WOMAN: It seems there is a lot of sewing happening in there.

Suddenly they both run for the chair. THE LADY *gets there first and sits.*

WOMAN: It is my turn.

LADY: What?

WOMAN: To sit. It is my turn.

LADY: How do you know it is your turn?

WOMAN: I have been counting the hours you have been sitting there. I've got to sit too now.

LADY: Let me just finish my make-up, okay? Then I'll let you sit.

She begins to make herself up again.

WOMAN: You lay it a bit thick, don't you?

LADY: What?

WOMAN: The make-up.

LADY: What would you know about it?

WOMAN: I am not stupid. I've got eyes, and I can see layers and layers of thick gooey stuff all over your face. [THE LADY *laughs mockingly*] It makes you look like a whore.

7

LADY: I *am* a whore.

WOMAN: You mean you are . . .

LADY: Of course. At least that's what people like you call us. But that's not why I use this stuff. People use it generally, you know, to improve their looks. I am sure even where you come from people use it.

WOMAN: But not as thick as that. You look like a ghost.

LADY: Not like a whore this time, eh?

WOMAN: Well, I am sorry. Maybe it was not the right thing to say.

LADY: Don't be sorry. I ply my trade openly. Everyone knows me in town. But, you see, to put you at ease – for you seem concerned with the thickness of my make-up – contrary to what many of you civilians may believe. I wear it thick because my skin is in a mess. Messed up by the follies of youth.

WOMAN: I can see that. Not the follies of youth, I mean. The skin.

LADY: Yeah it's in a mess. Got messed up when I was a little girl. You remember the skin lightening creams we used, eh?

WOMAN: Very well. *Ambi Extra, Artra* . . .

LADY: *Super Rose* and all the rest. When we were girls we used them, 'cause we wanted to be white. We bloody hated ourselves, so we used them. They've got something called hydroquinone in them, but we didn't know it then. All we wanted was to have white skins. Hydroquinone, sister woman, it destroys your skin.

WOMAN: Sister woman?

LADY: That's what I call all my girl friends. They call me that as well. Anyway it eats your skin. I was lucky. It didn't eat much of mine.

8

WOMAN: Yeah. I have seen people whose skins are completely destroyed. The whole face!

LADY: So that's why I use this stuff. To hide all the ugly blemishes. [*She has finished her make-up*] There! You see! As good as new. You should try some of this stuff too.

WOMAN: No thanks.

LADY: How old are you?

WOMAN: About forty.

LADY: See what I mean? We are about the same age, but look at you. Frumpy!

WOMAN: I think I am all right the way I am.

LADY: You think so. But do other people think so? We are not so selfish as to look beautiful for our own selves, you know. We do it for other people, so that they should have something to admire.

WOMAN: I think you have finished your make-up now.

LADY: Of course.

WOMAN: So let me sit on the chair.

[THE LADY *reluctantly stands up, and* THE WOMAN *sits*] Phew! I thought I'd never sit.

LADY: I don't like standing up for long periods. It's not good for my figure. I don't think this is a good arrangement.

WOMAN: It was a good arrangement when you ate my food. A single hand cannot wash itself, you said. Two hands clean each other.

LADY: I am not complaining.

THE WOMAN *takes the little packet left by* THE LADY *and begins to eat.*

WOMAN: So you knew we're going to be here for days.

LADY: Not really.

WOMAN: Then how come you brought a chair with you?

LADY: Because I know that the wheels of government move slowly.

WOMAN: Maybe you'll explain that.

LADY: I can see you are new to this country.

WOMAN: I was born here.

LADY: But you don't live here, I am sure.

WOMAN: Well, I work in Cape Town. In Mowbray. I am a flat cleaner there.

LADY: That's why you are not used to the waiting game. I have lived here all my life. I know about the waiting game. You are a novice. An absolute amateur.

WOMAN: I think I am beginning to know about the waiting game.

LADY: You don't know half the story. Let me tell you. When I go to the post office to buy a stamp, I take my chair with me. When I go to the bank to draw money – I used to have a respectable balance in my account, by the way – I take my chair with me. Why, because I know there is going to be a lot of waiting there. When I go to government offices for any service whatsoever I know I have to wait while bureaucrats have endless conversations about their lovers, and the great parties they have been attending lately. You go to these offices, sister woman, and the particular person who has been assigned to deal with your particular case has gone out. No one knows where. So you wait. Or they can't locate the file. Or perhaps the person who has to sign something has gone to a meeting somewhere. They always go to meetings. So you wait. I tell you, sister woman, all of us spend ninety-five percent of our waking hours waiting. Sooner or later this nation will learn from me. [*Shouting*] Bring your own chairs with you, and let's relax while waiting for something to happen! So you see why I am not very much amused when I have to share my chair with you?

10

WOMAN [*apologetically*]: It's just that it rained.

LADY: Another lesson in this waiting game. Get drip-dry clothes. You know, wash-and-wear. You never know when it's going to rain while you wait in some line. Look at the mess you are in, just because it rained like shit on us, and your clothes are all shrivelled up. Look at me. As fine as ever.

WOMAN: When it gets dry I won't need your chair. I'll sit flat on the ground, and keep my place on the queue. See who's going to feed you.

LADY: Ha! It won't get dry. Rain never behaves that way. As long as we are waiting here, it's going to rain every time and the ground won't dry up.

The sound of the gong.

WOMAN: The workers are coming back. The storekeepers and the office girls in their beautiful dresses.

LADY [*shouting*]: We hope you had a lovely lunch, and God bless you. [*They both stand up and raise their arms as if in supplication*] We greet you, our lords and masters!

WOMAN: And our ladies too!

LADY: *Marena!*

WOMAN: *Nkosi yamakhosi!*

LADY: *Melimo ea lefats'e!*

Lights gradually fade to black.

Scene 2

THE LADY *and* THE WOMAN. *Still on the queue.* THE WOMAN *is sitting on the chair, and* THE LADY *is impatiently pacing the floor.*

LADY: It is the inertia that kills me.

WOMAN: What's that?

LADY: Inactivity.

WOMAN: We could kill time by playing some game.

LADY: Like what?

WOMAN: *Liketo.* We could get some small stones and play *liketo.*

LADY: On this wet ground?

WOMAN: I forgot about that. The wet ground. We could devise a game. Something we can play while one of us is sitting on the chair and the other one is standing up.

LADY: Maybe we could lay every guy on this queue.

WOMAN [*standing up and horrified*]: What!

LADY: Lay them, you know. The poor guys have been standing here for days, and I am sure quite a few of them are horny. We could all have a ball.

WOMAN: I think that's disgusting.

LADY [*with relish*]: Yeah, let's all be disgusting.

WOMAN: But then, it's something you are used to. It's your profession, you said.

LADY: Just for kicks this time. We wouldn't dream of charging these wretched souls a cent.

WOMAN: Why did you become a prostitute?

LADY: Eh?

WOMAN: You heard me.

LADY: You expect a sob story, I am sure. A broken home. Abused as a child by a step-father. Family so poor we had to scrounge for food any way and anywhere we could. I am sorry to disappoint you. I was from a very happy family. We were not millionaires, but we had enough to eat. You can even say we lived almost on the wealthy side of the street. I went to a private school. Even up to university. Attempted a BA. Didn't finish though.

WOMAN: Then why did you become a prostitute?

LADY: Choice! Godammit, can't a woman choose what she wants to do with her life?

WOMAN: You are such a beautiful woman. You could have made some lucky man a good wife.

LADY: I did make somebody a good wife. I was so damn good that he left me. Ran away with the maid.

THE WOMAN *has seen something which excites her.*

WOMAN: Look, they are loading it into the trucks!

LADY: What?

WOMAN: The fucken rice we are waiting for. They are loading it into those trucks.

LADY: Don't worry. They'll surely leave something for us.

WOMAN: It's not fair! We have been waiting here for days, and those trucks just drive in and get loaded with rice. It's not fair!

13

LADY: They'll leave some bags for us, I tell you. I am sure they have counted the number of people in the queue and they'll leave some bags for us.

WOMAN: That's not what concerns me, er . . . sister woman, as you say you're called.

LADY: Yeah, sister woman!

WOMAN: That's not what concerns me. You see all those trucks? They have the names of different companies written on them. Wholesalers, general dealers and jobbers. They're buying all this rice here because it's cheap. They're going to sell it in their shops. At a very high price.

LADY: So what? They're in business.

WOMAN [*shouting at the trucks*]: Fuck you all, big-bellied businessmen. That is our rice!

LADY [*trying to stop her*]: Shut up, for God's sake. You are going to make things worse for us. They are going to keep us waiting here for the next ten days just for that.

WOMAN: Listen, we have rights as well as any person here. We have been waiting for days. And these big men with big trucks just push in and load the rice.

LADY: Nobody forced you to come here, you know that. Nobody said, 'Sister woman, you are forced to go and buy rice from the government food aid depots. Go or face the firing squad!'

WOMAN: If it's food aid it must be given to the poor for free. And in many cases it helps to keep them where they are – poor.

LADY: The poor, yes, and you and I don't qualify. Let's face it, you came because you heard it's a bargain. You knew before you came that the countries that donated it meant for it to be distributed among the poor for free. But you came to buy it still. You shout at those big guys, but you are not different from them.

WOMAN: Do you have to bundle me with them?

LADY: All we need is patience, and our turn will come.

WOMAN: Where does this rice come from anyway?

LADY: Italy. You see the writing on all those bags? It's in Italian. I can read it because I was once married to an Italian chef. I learned a little bit of the language.

WOMAN: You have been doing a lot of marrying it seems.

LADY: Only once. Never got married again.

WOMAN: What about the man who ran away with the maid?

LADY: That's the same Italian chef. When I met him I was a student at the university. He had a restaurant just outside the gate of the main campus. My friends and I used to eat and drink there while at the same time competing about who was going to catch him first. I won. We lived together and for a while I was a queen. He took me to places and spent good money on me. We went to Mauritius. We went to all the gambling dens you can think of. We went to Sun City.

WOMAN: And now you have nothing to show for it?

LADY: A daughter. A good-for-nothing teenage daughter. She gets laid all over town and doesn't bring a cent home. Spends it all on herself. Flashy clothes and jewellery.

WOMAN: You are in the same trade then?

LADY: Same trade? Sister woman, I taught that girl everything she knows. Every little trick. Every little movement. The ungrateful brat!

The gong.

LADY: It is time up! They are going home for the day.

WOMAN: They can't do that without serving us.

LADY: It's four-thirty, sister woman. they're knocking off.

WOMAN: All this sister woman rubbish! It irritates me, you know that?

15

LADY: I don't see why it should. I think it's nice. We got it from some black American customers who once came here years back.

WOMAN: Well, I hope you'll stop calling me that.

LADY: I don't see why you should be irritable. It's not my fault that these people are going home without serving us. Ah, there they are coming. Let's greet them nicely. It humours them.

THE WOMAN *sits down on the chair.*

WOMAN: I am not going to do that. I am sick and tired of kowtowing to these bastards who don't have any regard for us.

THE LADY *waves feebly.*

LADY [*wanly*]: Good night, my lords and masters. Do have sweet dreams.

WOMAN: I say let them all go and fry in hell.

LADY: Sh... They'll hear you.

WOMAN: Of course I want them to hear me.

LADY: Shit, why did I sit with you here?

WOMAN: We both didn't have any choice. We are in a queue.

LADY: Listen, I know the system, okay? You just come from Cape Town and you want to mess up everything for everybody. Those people are civil servants, do you hear that? You don't just talk to them as though they are the woman who sells fat cakes at the street corner.

WOMAN: Listen, I think I am going home now.

LADY: Why? You don't want the rice any more?

WOMAN: I need the rice, but I am not prepared to wallow in degradation for it.

LADY: Well, if you think you are a better buttock than all these people who have been waiting here who am I to stop you?

16

WOMAN: Indeed who are you to stop me. Okay, it was nice meeting you. I must go now.

She makes to go.

LADY: Sister woman, wait! what will your children eat?

WOMAN: I'll just have to buy for them in the shop. It's more expensive there of course, but what choice do I have?

LADY: You have been waiting here for many days. Surely you can wait for another night. I am sure in the morning they'll serve us.

WOMAN: You have been saying that from the very first day we met. I am sure when they come back from lunch, they'll serve us. I am sure ... I am sure ... I am sick and tired of all that. I must go now.

LADY [*appealingly*]: Please, sister woman. Don't go. Listen, I'll even let you use my chair for ever. Bequeath it to you. Only please don't go now.

THE LADY *holds* THE WOMAN *tight in an attempt to stop her from going.* THE WOMAN *tries to break loose.*

WOMAN: Let go of me, bloody whore! What do you want from me, eh? What is it that you want from me?

LADY [*pleading*]: Please don't go. How am I going to live without you? [*She kneels*] Look, I am kneeling down on the wet ground in my beautiful dress pleading and begging.

WOMAN: I thought as much. It is my money you are so much interested in. If I go you'll have to find another victim who'll buy you meals while you wait in your perpetual queue.

LADY [*standing up and mustering as much dignity as she can*]: I am broke. I don't have a cent to my name. The only money I have is the ten bucks with which I'll pay for the rice. That's all.

WOMAN [*coming back*]: But you led me to believe you were a prosperous street walker.

LADY [*greatly offended*]: I am not a street walker. I have never stood at street corners waiting for clients to come and pick me up in their cars. No one can claim to have ever seen me in front of the Victoria Hotel soliciting for the clientele. I am not an orphan of the night. I am a courtesan. A courtesan, do you hear that?

WOMAN: Okay, I am sorry. You are a courtesan, whatever that means.

LADY: It means that my clients are from the upper crust of the society. I entertain Ministers and Ambassadors. I am a high class hooker. I service rich capitalists when they come to town on business.

WOMAN: Then what are you doing on this queue with low-lives like us?

LADY: I am broke, I told you.

WOMAN: Courtesans don't make enough to make ends meet these days?

LADY [*breaking down and weeping uncontrollably*]: Oh, sister woman. I am old. I don't know what to do.

WOMAN [*trying to comfort her*]: You are not old. You're only forty. You are still a beautiful woman.

LADY: They don't come any more. The johns don't come any more.

WOMAN: Johns?

LADY: The clients. The customers. The johns. The young girls have taken over. Teenage whores line the streets by the dozen, and no one wants to screw us old whores any more. The competition is hard, sister woman, very hard. And now we are dying of hunger.

WOMAN: And you've read books, and you've a lot of learning. You could have easily become like one of the office girls who have been coming in and out of this yard in their beautiful Sunday dresses.

LADY [*pride taking over again*]: What's the difference? Many of them have to sleep with someone to get their jobs. They have to lay some dirty old man to get a promotion. We are in the same profession, sister woman. Only I do it openly and on my terms, as a free agent. They get laid and still have to sit behind office desks and typewriters before they can get their porridge. [*She looks at herself in the compact mirror*] Oh damn, the tears have messed up my make-up.

WOMAN: Don't worry. Nobody will notice. It's getting to be night anyway. You'll do it again in the morning.

LADY: Honestly, do you think I am old, sister woman?

WOMAN: Forty is never old.

LADY: Then why don't they come, sister woman? Why don't the customers come any more? I am not ugly. I am still beautiful. Look at my body. *U ntse u lutlisa mathe.* Why the hell don't these bastards come, sister woman?

WOMAN: As you say, there is all this young blood now. Like your daughter.

LADY [*desperately*]: Am I old, sister woman? Am I ugly?

WOMAN [*reassuringly*]: Not at all. It's just that men are fickle. That's the whole problem.

LADY: Yes, the bastards are unreliable. They find you when you are nice and fresh and young. They use you in many different ways, and then throw you away like the marrow of a horse when they have drained you of all flesh and blood. I hate the bastards. I was young once, sister woman. I was young and beautiful. I was the campus queen. That's when the father of my daughter met me. He lavished all his love and money on me. I always had booze and cigarettes for myself and my friends. I even left varsity for him. I gave birth to his daughter. Then the bastard left

19

me. I heard he got a job as chief chef on some luxury liner.

WOMAN: Maybe that's because he was a foreigner. You should have got yourself a local man and settled down.

LADY: Local men? They are bastards as well. Maybe even worse. They take you for granted. They don't treat you like a lady. They treat you like scum and you got to be at their back and call. Do everything for them. Even have to wipe their arses. No, sister woman. Men are all the same. That is why I got into this profession. I have been used. So I use them. The men I sleep with, in them I see the Italian chef. All of them are representative of him. That is why I am going to lay them to death, and take their money to boot. I hate the bastards, sister woman.

WOMAN: Yet you make love to them.

LADY: Those are johns. They are not human beings. Even as they undress I look at them and I feel like spitting all over their shrivelled bodies. I find them pathetic. Pathetic and disgusting creatures. I wish I had AIDS, then I'd spread it like wild fire. Kill all the bastards.

WOMAN: We are all victims of a social order that allows this to happen. But I don't think yours is the solution.

LADY: What would you know about it? You went to Cape Town to work for the Boers. Clean after their filth.

WOMAN: Look at you now. All scared and worried because the johns don't come any more. That's the problem with your kind of job. Old age comes quite early. And there is no insurance against that.

LADY: There is insurance. It's just that I was unfortunate, things didn't work out for me. I thought my daughter would be my insurance in my old age. You should see her, she is a beautiful little thing. An expert in the job, for she was trained by the best. But a good-for-nothing brat who doesn't care for her mama who brought her into the world and taught her all she knows. One of the major insurance policies, of course, is marriage. All of us, as we do our rounds, we are looking for a john who will fall head over heels, and marry. There are many of us who are married all over Europe, married by former clients who wanted to keep this thing for themselves forever. Married by European businessmen, contractors, engineers, aid workers and so on, who initially came here as experts sent by their governments, or as tourists. The women now lead respectable lives as housewives. Others have forged careers for themselves. Only a few days ago I met one of my old colleagues. She is visiting home, you know, from Switzerland where she has a successful marriage and a successful career as a singer. She sings gospel music all over the place. Sometimes she gets invited to sing in anti-apartheid rallies all over Europe. You can't get more respectable than that. No one would ever know about her past. Except for the fact that she is saved. Not only does she sing gospel all over the show, she preaches it as well, and tells everyone she was once a hooker.

WOMAN: I am sure she is the same person I saw the other day. They told me she used to be a call girl, then she got married in Europe and got saved.

LADY: She must be the one, sister woman. She goes to the Victoria and preaches to the ladies of the night.

WOMAN [*preaching*]: My sisters, my sisters in the Lord. Isn't it a wonderful feeling to know that someone's blood did flow?

THE LADY *is now the preacher's audience. She sits down on the ground. Sometimes she will stand up as the spirit moves her. Lights dim, for it is now night.*

LADY: Yes. It is our blood. Very inconveniencing when one is on duty.

21

WOMAN: I am talking about the blood of Jesus Christ our Lord. The blood that flowed to save us from our sins. The blood that shows to one and all how much the Lord loves us. It is love that I am talking about, my sisters of the night. Not the love of the flesh. But the love that is everlasting.

LADY: Amen! Hallelujah!

WOMAN: I am talking now about repentance. Repentance from our sins. Once upon a time, I was like you. I moved from hotel to hotel trying to get men. I jumped from bed to bed. I used to sell my body on the altar of Satan. I used to be a harlot of Sodom and Gomorrah. Then one day I saw the light. [*She sings a hymn.* THE LADY *joins, and they both dance and clap their hands. It is obvious that the spirit has moved them.*] I saw the light, sisters of the night.

LADY: Amen.

WOMAN: Jesus spoke to me. He said: 'My daughter, I gave you your body, and it is the temple of the Lord. *Hobaneng joale ha u ntse u fana ka eona hohle moo?*' I used to lead the same kind of life. But I got saved. Now I live in my villa in Geneva, and I praise the Lord all the time. I urge you to repent. I urge you to be saved! Do I see repentance, my sisters of the night?

LADY: Amen!

WOMAN: Do I see signs of repentance?

LADY [*greatly moved by the spirit*]: I will repent. I feel the spirit. I will repent. But first let me find myself a john who will marry me and take me to Europe with him, or who will build me a house in Maseru West, and furnish it. Then I'll repent! And be saved! And work for the Lord . . .

Overcome by the spirit, THE LADY *collapses. Lights fall to black.*

Scene 3

The queue. THE LADY *is now sitting on the ground and is smoking a cigarette. She is dishevelled and is no longer fussing about her looks.* THE WOMAN *looks as she did in the previous scenes: simple and neat. She is whistling or humming the hymn of the previous scene.*

LADY: I wish you'd stop that. It irritates me.

WOMAN: You can have your chair. You don't have to sit on the wet ground.

LADY: You don't have to patronise me.

WOMAN: It is your chair after all.

LADY: I don't care any more. I can sit anywhere I want. I can even lie flat on my belly in that mud puddle. It is not your business at all.

WOMAN: Well, if it suits you.

LADY: You are gloating.

WOMAN: About what?

LADY [*bitterly*]: Now that you know so much about me you think you can sit in judgement.

WOMAN: I didn't say anything.

LADY: I can see you. You think I am going to allow you to pity me, and to patronise me. You are Miss Perfect and I am a fallen whore.

WOMAN: If it will make you happy, let me tell you that I am not perfect.

LADY: How's that?

WOMAN: When I went to Cape Town for the first time it was with a man.

LADY: So what's wrong with that?

WOMAN: He was my boss.

LADY: Yeah?

WOMAN: I ran away with my boss to Cape Town. He was a young man *oa Letaliana*. I was his maid. I looked after his house while he ran his restaurant business.

LADY: See how strange life is?

WOMAN: He was a philanderer, *Letaliana leo*. Brought different women home every day. Mostly ladies of the night. But oh, he was charming, with an impish sense of humour. It was the easiest thing to fall in love with him.

LADY: Same with mine. These *Mataliana* are all like that it seems.

WOMAN: Yeah. Then he made one of his many women pregnant, and decided to live with her. I couldn't bear another woman living permanently in that house, and I told him I was quitting. He wouldn't hear of it. [*Mimicking Italian accent*] I cannot live without you, *ausi.* Let us run away to Cape Town. I have many brothers there. They will get me a job in a nice big hotel. His business was not doing well. In fact he had gone bankrupt. So we ran away to Cape Town.

THE LADY *is engrossed in the story. She sits still, one hand on her cheek, looking fixedly at* THE WOMAN.

WOMAN: My first trip to South Africa, and I was with a white man. It was before they had scrapped the Immorality Act, so I passed as his maid. Which in any case I

24

was, besides the fact that we were lovers also. We drove to Cape Town and got ourselves a flat in Mowbray – one of those self-contained flats where they supply you with everything, including kitchen utensils. For a while we were very happy, although at every knock at the door we would jump: 'Police!' Then one day he says: 'Dammit, we can't live like this, like animals in a cage.' I tell him: 'But you knew when we came here that there are strange laws in this country.'

'Yeah, I knew, but I didn't think it would be so bad.'

'So let's go back home.'

'Where is home?'

'Where you took me from.'

'My home is in Italy.'

We forgot about the whole thing, and were happy again for a while. Then one day he didn't come back. Just disappeared like a fart in the wind. He had left in the morning to meet his 'brothers' to talk about a job. He didn't come back. [*Screaming*] What am I going to do? Please, what am I going to do? I stayed for a few days and the groceries ran out. The complex manager kept on phoning me about due rent. [*Screaming again*] I don't know where he is! I don't have any money so I can't pay rent! Please try to understand! Meanwhile I was desperately trying to phone the numbers he used to phone. [*Shouting on the imaginary phone*] Where the hell is this man? Tell me, didn't he tell you where he was going? Didn't he leave a message for me? A tiny little message, anything? But no one knew, or maybe they didn't want to tell. Until at last one of his 'brothers' told me. He'd got a job as a cook on a ship. The ship had sailed to Hong Kong days ago. Meanwhile the manager of the flats wanted his rent. So I had to work there for months, cleaning the flats, in order to pay him back. Well, even after I had paid him back, I decided to stay and continue working.

LADY [*sadly*]: See what I told you, sister woman. Men always do these things to us. The scum!

WOMAN: I just want you to know that I don't live in the past. What happened happened and I remember it only in so far as it is a lesson learnt never to be repeated.

LADY: You are not bitter then?

WOMAN: I have no time for bitterness. I rebuilt from the ashes. Got myself a small room in one of the locations. I have a regular job as a flat cleaner. Mind you, I am not saying things are easy. We are struggling on. Like everyone else.

LADY: So they pay you well as a flat cleaner?

WOMAN: That's one of the things we struggle about. I am a member of the Domestic Workers Union. We struggle for better wages and better working conditions. Things are still bad, but we are going to win.

LADY: I know about these unions. It's politics, that's what it is.

WOMAN: Is it not through politics that the laws that have created these terrible conditions for us are made?

LADY: They are not our politics. They are politics of another country.

WOMAN: I work there so everything that happens there affects me. It affects you too, although you've, like most others, decided to wear blinkers and pretend that you live in a never-never land that will smoothly map out its destiny irrespective of all the turbulence surrounding it. One day it's going to dawn on you, and on the rest of all the others who think like you, that this struggle is not just South African. It is Southern African.

LADY [*taken aback*]: My God, you stand with a person in a queue for the whole four days and you think you know them! You are an agitator, and you won't survive here if I must tell you.

WOMAN [*laughs mockingly*]: That's what they call us over there too. Agitators! It is as if when you are forced to sit on a hot coal stove someone else must come and teach you that your buttocks are burning. I tell you, my working there has put me through a baptism of fire. I won't sit back and take abuse from anyone. That is what I have been trying to tell you. You don't have to take abuse from anyone.

LADY: Hey, who says I take abuse? Just because I have patience and I take my chair with me doesn't mean I take abuse.

WOMAN: It is now time for us to change things. To liberate not only ourselves, but the men themselves, for we are all in bondage! Yes, the men in this free and independent country are in bondage, mostly to their attitudes. That is why you see them sitting back and swimming in the glories of the past. Oh, our ancestors were great! They defended this country against all sorts of invaders! Oh, we are descendants of the great warriors who through their wisdom created this nation. That is all they ever do. We do not see much of what they are doing for the future. It is as if the past will take care of the future without any effort from the present.

LADY: Look, I think all these things you say are making me uncomfortable. People here don't just say things like these in public places – particularly when we are waiting here to be served. But what I don't understand is you say you don't take any abuse, but you have been waiting here with the rest of us.

27

WOMAN [*laughs*]: Through your persuasion. But frankly though, I suffer from the same disease from which we all seem to suffer. We say: Well, this is home, we are prepared to accept shoddiness. We are still a young nation so these things are expected to happen. In other words what we are saying is that we don't think we are capable of producing the best results, so we are prepared to tolerate inefficiency and corruption.

LADY: Sister woman, I think you have gone through a lot of pain in that place where you work. And I have been sitting here thinking that it was the end of the world for me just because the johns don't come any more. I feel such a fool.

WOMAN: You are not a fool at all. And yes there has been a lot of pain. But there has been hope as well. Sometimes hope in death. There is a coloured woman I work with. I was visiting her one day in her location when we saw her son being gunned down by the police. In cold blood. She ran to her son and knelt down by his side. When mothers whose sons have been ripped to pieces by bullets are able to say 'My son's death is a victory for the people. He wasn't just mine. He belonged to the people.' Then you know that victory is indeed certain, and liberation day is just around the corner. [*Laughing*] Now, I know you will tell me that these are their politics and not ours. Perhaps you think that when bullets fly they choose!

LADY: I am sorry, sister woman.

WOMAN: About what?

LADY: I don't know. I just feel that I have got to be sorry about something.

The gong.

WOMAN: Ah, they are coming back to work.

LADY: Should I greet them, sister woman?

WOMAN: It is up to you.

LADY: Are you going to greet them yourself?

WOMAN: No, they do not deserve it.

LADY: Then I won't greet them too.

They watch the throngs as they pass. THE WOMAN *has a contemptuous look.*

WOMAN: Jealous down, the office girls do look lovely in their summer dresses.

LADY: I don't want to seem disagreeable, sister woman, but you don't know much about summer dresses. To you those are beautiful because you don't have much expertise on clothing. You can tell me about your politics, but leave fashion to me. Now, if you are talking of cloth, you are talking of me. Even now that I don't earn anything you can see that I haven't lost my taste for a good cloth. I could have been a model. Don't you think I could have been a model, sister woman?

WOMAN: You are all mud now, so it's hard to tell.

LADY: Jealous down, sister woman.

WOMAN: Well, I might not know much about fashion, but I notice that people in your profession tend to be more on the fancy side.

LADY: It's only when we go out to work. We have to be recognisable to prospective clients. At the same time we have to be sexually attractive – physically I mean. It's all part of the job. Like a uniform or something. When we are not at work we change. [*With nostalgia*] I remember in the past – I doubt if the current generation still does that – we used to choose a day each week when we would all don our Sunday dresses and we would take our regular lovers and husbands for a night out in town. On this day,

29

even if the wealthiest johns came to town and wanted to do business, we turned them down, for this was the day for our lovers and husbands.

[*There is a pause. Each of the two women is lost in thought. Then there is a sudden outburst of rebelliousness from* THE LADY. *She goes to* THE WOMAN *in a very challenging manner. She is in a fighting mood.*]

You are a flat cleaner in Cape Town. All sorts of men go there with their mistresses and with the likes of us. You clean their filth! You are not better off!

Lights fade to black.

Scene 4

It is dawn. The two women are still in the queue. THE WOMAN *is sleeping on the chair.* THE LADY *stands hovering over her.*

LADY: Sister woman.

WOMAN: What is it?

LADY: Are you awake?

WOMAN: No, I am asleep.

LADY: It's a new day today.

WOMAN: Every day is a new day.

LADY: I feel something very important is going to happen today.

WOMAN: Congratulations.

LADY: For what?

WOMAN: For feeling something important is going to happen today. Now let me sleep, okay?

THE LADY *walks around for a few paces, then goes back to* THE WOMAN.

LADY: Sister woman.

WOMAN: What now?

LADY: I am sorry I attacked you yesterday.

WOMAN: I understand.

LADY: What do you understand?

WOMAN: Well, I think you were under some kind of pressure.

LADY: You know, one other thing I hate about you, sister woman, is that you always pretend to be some kind of saint. You are a hypocrite. I hate hypocrites, sister woman.

WOMAN: Thank you.

THE LADY *wakes* THE WOMAN *up violently.*

LADY: Don't thank me, dammit. Listen, I attacked you. I attacked you for no apparent reason. And all you can say is: 'I understand' and 'Thank you'.

WOMAN: What do you want me to do then?

LADY: Slap me! Kick me! Whatever!

WOMAN: Listen I am tired, and I am not at all prepared to argue with you. Especially at this ungodly hour.

LADY: You are a hypocrite, that's what you are. You are a wishy-washy liberal. And I hate liberals. Come here! [*The two women stand facing each other.*] Slap me.

WOMAN: What for?

LADY: To defend yourself.

WOMAN: Against what?

LADY: Against me. I attacked you last night, remember?

WOMAN: That was last night.

LADY: And what did you do about it?

WOMAN: I could have beaten sense into you if I wanted to. In fact the way you have been carrying on, I should have done that a long time ago. But what would be the point?

LADY: There you start patronising me again.

WOMAN: You talk about defending oneself. You don't know a thing about that. Otherwise you'd not be carrying your chair with you everywhere you go.

LADY: What's my chair got to do with it?

32

WOMAN: Everything. When they violate you, you wait. You patiently wait until such time that they come around to doing something about it. You have the patience of a saint. When they violate you, you avenge yourself by laying men all over the place. Then you hope things will be all right.

LADY: For me certainly. I get the satisfaction of making them pay – draining their blood and money.

WOMAN: And presto! The world has changed. Injustice has been eradicated! The unequal distribution of the country's wealth has been remedied! Bureaucratic red tape has been eliminated and nobody has to stand on the queue for days on end any more!

LADY: What do you want me to do then, Miss Politician? What have you done yourself?

WOMAN: Not much. But we should demand a change and be willing to suffer for it, rather than suffer in silence as we have been doing here. Tell me, why are we still here? Why are we still waiting? We are even fighting over the use of the chair. Because we are waiting. Life passes by and we are onlookers. We are like the sedated who slept through a revolution.

LADY [*determined*]: I was never an onlooker. I am all action. When the revolution comes I want to carry a gun. I don't sit on the sidelines and darn socks for the fighters.

WOMAN: It is here already.

LADY: Well, I haven't seen much of it. I am still waiting for it, and when it comes . . .

WOMAN: You don't wait for a revolution. You make it happen.

LADY [*carried away*]: No, I don't sit on the sidelines and sing songs and ululate with *melilietsane* to make the blood

33

of men boil so that they may bravely march into battle. I carry the gun. I march into battle.

WOMAN: There is hope for all of us yet.

The gong.

LADY: They come again in their Sunday dresses.

WOMAN: Sunday dresses, and summer dresses. That's the same thing then?

LADY: There are winter Sunday dresses and there are summer Sunday dresses.

WOMAN: I never had summer dresses and winter dresses. I just had dresses. I don't have special dresses that I wear on Sundays.

LADY: Sunday dresses are not only worn on Sundays. They are worn on any day when one wants to look beautiful. That is why you see the office girls in their Sunday dresses.

The gong again, repeatedly.

WOMAN: What's that now? Don't tell me they are going back to lunch just after coming in.

LADY: Look, there is a man with a megaphone. He is going to address us.

They listen.

WOMAN: What's he saying?

LADY: He says we must keep order in our queue. Aha, he says rice is now ready. No pushing. We must move in an orderly manner to the window over there.

WOMAN: At last! Let us move with the queue.

LADY: Should we really?

WOMAN: That's what we have been waiting for, is it not?

LADY: Yeah. For all these days.

WOMAN: So let's get moving.

LADY: To that window.

WOMAN: And what happens there?

LADY: We fill in the forms. Come, '*mè*, come! We don't have all day to deal with you.

THE WOMAN *is now a rice buying customer and* THE LADY *an office girl.*

> Are you going to talk or not? Why do you just stand there staring at me as if you have just swallowed a rat?

WOMAN: I have come to buy rice, '*mè*.

LADY: Of course that's what we sell here. You have come to buy all the rice in this depot?

WOMAN: No, just one bag.

LADY: So, why don't you say so? You people like wasting time. Do I have to prompt you all the time?

WOMAN: One bag of rice, please '*mè*. And here is the money.

LADY: You don't pay at this window. Here we only fill in the forms, in triplicate, then you go and join the other queue where you pay. Is that clear?

WOMAN: It is clear.

LADY: Good. You will fill in your name here. But there is more information that we need from you before we can sell you a bag of rice. You see, here I need to fill in your age, and on this line your place of birth. Place and date of birth actually. Then here of course I fill in your sex. Male or female?

WOMAN: Female, '*mè*.

LADY: Good, now here you fill in ... You can write, can you?

WOMAN: Yes.

LADY: Then you can fill in the information yourself while I finish eating my fat cake. But first of all let me show you the other information that we need. Here you fill in the colour of your eyes.

WOMAN: For buying rice?

LADY: The government needs all this information. Colour of your eyes here. On this line colour of your hair. And here your height and weight. On this line you fill in, as you can see, the number of teeth in your mouth.

WOMAN: I don't know. I haven't counted them.

LADY: You'll have to count them. You can pay our messenger fifty cents and he'll count them for you. On this line here you fill in whether you have had any communicable diseases or not, and of course here we need your address and telephone number. Name and address of your next of kin here.

WOMAN: Is that all.

LADY: That will be all for now. Next!

WOMAN: Wait. But where do I go from here.

LADY: '*Mè*, I don't have the whole day to waste on you. I told you to join the other queue at that window. That is where you pay.

WOMAN: Then I get the rice?

LADY: Not yet. You have to go to the third window where they will stamp your papers with a rubber stamp.

WOMAN: Then finally . . .

LADY: After that you have to join the other queue where you will present your papers to the Right Honourable the Keeper of the Stores. He will assign you a person with whom you'll go to choose your bag of rice. Then of course you've got to sign for it.

[*They discard their roles as office girl and customer.*]

That, sister woman, is what we'll go through.

WOMAN: At least now everything will be over and done away with.

LADY: I am not going through with it.

WOMAN: You are not

LADY: No. I am not. I am going home now, and I am not taking the chair.

WOMAN: What about the rice?

LADY: To hell with the rice! I am going home, and I know that never again will I need the food-aid rice, and my chair of patience. Are you coming or not?

WOMAN [*excitedly*]: You know what? I love you. I think you are a great human being. Of course I am coming. I am coming.

LADY: Let's go then.

They make to go. There is a great warmth between them. They hold each other's hands and there is a pause for a while.

LADY: Sister woman, do you ever think about him?

WOMAN: Who?

LADY: The man.

WOMAN: The man I ran away with? Yeah, sometimes.

LADY: The man who left me. Sometimes.

WOMAN: Well, mine left me too.

LADY: Men . . . They are the same. They are like children of one person.

Lights fade to black as the two women go out.

THE FINAL DANCE

A script for a cinepoem

Fade in

Ext street – early morning

This is more of an alley than a street. Very filthy. There are bits of trash all over: cans, empty milk cartons and so on. There are two overflowing garbage cans, and another one fallen down, most of its contents gracing the street. A thin stream of dirty water runs down the street, past the garbage cans and out of the frame.

Closer angle – the fallen garbage can

There is a dog inside which causes the can to rock from side to side as it tries to select what is and is not worth eating. It finds some juicy morsel and, in its enthusiasm rocks the garbage can so much that it rolls and knocks against one of the upright garbage cans. The resulting clanking sound startles the dog which runs out of the garbage can.

Follow – DOG

It is scared to death and runs up the street whining.

Ext a shack – Same early morning

The shack is roughly built: a collage of wood, corrugated iron, cardboard and what have you. A narrow street passes in front of it and along the street runs the thin stream of dirty water we saw earlier. The running dog approaches, still whining, and coils itself at the doorstep. It gives three barks, and an OLD MAN opens the door from inside. It walks into the shack.

Int the shack – same morning
The DOG walks in and the OLD MAN closes the door. The shack is sparsely furnished, mostly with makeshift furniture: a table, a bed, a conglomeration of boxes and a wheelbarrow. Although one can see that an attempt has been made to keep the room clean, it is too crammed to look neat. There is a pile of aluminium containers – mostly beverage cans – in one corner. The only sign of luxury in the whole room is a stereo set.

Closer angle – A CAT
It is peacefully sleeping under the makeshift table.

Resume – OLD MAN
He goes to the stereo and plays a record. It is Kabalevsky's 'Comedians' Gallop'. He improvises a clownish dance and sweeps across the room to a dilapidated cabinet in the other corner. He opens the cabinet, still dancing his awkward dance, takes out a carton of milk, dances to the table from under which he pulls a saucepan. He pours the milk into the saucepan and puts it back under the table. The DOG and the CAT run to drink the milk.

Closer on DOG and CAT
They are noisily lapping the milk.

Resume – OLD MAN
He puts the cans in a sack and loads them on the wheelbarrow which he pushes to the door. He dances back to the stereo and stops the music, then dances back to the wheelbarrow and pushes it out of the door. The dog follows him out.

Ext shack – same morning
The OLD MAN walks out of the shack pushing his wheelbarrow into the street. The dog coils itself on the doorstep.

Int recycling centre – Late afternoon

A MAN is weighing aluminium cans on a scale.

Closer angle – A sign

**ALUMINIUM CANS AND NEWSPAPER RECYCLING CENTRE
– PRICES PER POUND**

There are illegible letters below that – presumably the prices.

Resume – MAN weighing the cans

The OLD MAN is unloading the cans, and the MAN is weighing them. He takes out some coins from his pocket and pays the OLD MAN who looks at them protestingly.

Closer on the OLD MAN's hand
Only three quarters.

Resume – MAN and OLD MAN

The man shrugs his shoulders and points at the weight-registering part of the scale. The old man pushes his wheelbarrow and walks away in disgust.

Ext the street – same afternoon

This is a small town street. Very few people. Once in a while an old car wheezes by. The OLD MAN is pushing his wheelbarrow. He sees a can lying on the sidewalk, picks it up and loads it on the wheelbarrow.

Follow OLD MAN

He has left the town now, and the road begins to change as he walks on. It is now a beautiful paved road, with wild shrubs and flowers growing on the sides. From his POV we see a white mansion at some distance – rising and looking almost like an old-world castle.

Ext mansion – same day

It is of imposing Gothic revival style. Strains of Strauss's 'Tales from the Vienna Woods' coming from within. There is a well tended and expertly landscaped garden.

Closer on one of the mansion's windows

Int a bedroom in the mansion – same day

A LITTLE GIRL of about ten sits alone in her bedroom. She is obviously very bored, and doesn't seem to know what to do with herself. Both the room's furnishings and her costume are of the Victorian era. As the door to her room opens and her NURSEMAID, also in Victorian attire, peeks in, strains of Strauss and sounds of laughter and gaiety become louder. The NURSEMAID nods her head and closes the door again. The LITTLE GIRL goes to the window and looks out.

Ext the paved path in front of the mansion – same day

The path is seen from the little girl's POV. The OLD MAN, pushing his wheelbarrow, passes by and looks up at the window.

CU – OLD MAN

He smiles at the GIRL and waves.

CU – GIRL

She waves back, and for the first time we see a gleam of happiness in her eyes.

Back to:
Int bedroom – same afternoon

The girl sneaks out of her bedroom.

Follow – GIRL

She walks through a long corridor, down the stairs into the ballroom.

Int ballroom – same afternoon

A ball is taking place. Ladies and gentlemen in their formal Victorian spendour are waltzing to Strauss, played by a chamber orchestra. The LITTLE GIRL sneaks out of the room.

Favour – a dancing couple

We shall later know that these are the parents of the LITTLE GIRL.

Ext mansion – same afternoon

The GIRL sneaks out of the door, runs to the OLD MAN, and looks at him curiously. Then she impishly pulls him away. The OLD MAN follows sheepishly.

Ext the garden – early evening

It is getting darker now. The OLD MAN and the GIRL are waltzing to the faint strains of Strauss. Although he tends to do the clownish dance of the Kabalevsky, she patiently teaches him the right steps.

Ext another part of the garden – same evening

The worried NURSEMAID, helped by a manservant or two, is looking for the GIRL.

Back to:
Two shot: OLD MAN *and* GIRL

They continue their dance. Then they stop. The GIRL pulls him towards the mansion. At first he resists, but the GIRL insists.

Int the ballroom – same evening

The waltz continues. The GIRL, with a mischievous twinkle in her eye and an obvious resolve to shock their Victorian graces, enters, pulling the embarrassed old man by the hand. She goes with him right to the centre of the room where they join the waltz. The LADIES and GENTLEMEN move back in disgust and consternation. They all stand on the sides of the room, and the OLD MAN and the GIRL take centre stage and dance.

Favour – the GIRL'S PARENTS

They are both horrified and embarrassed.

Back to:
Full shot – OLD MAN *and* GIRL

She dances away impishly, and the OLD MAN is lost in the enchantment of the moment. Not only does the raggedness of his clothes make him out of place here, but also the fact that they are of the 1990s.

Int the OLD MAN'S *shack – evening*

There has been a segue of Strauss with Kabalevsky, which is now playing on the stereo. The old man continues his dance as in the previous scene, although his partner is now imaginary. His CAT and DOG are the spectators.

Ext mansion – day

The OLD MAN sits on his wheelbarrow on the paved path outside the mansion and looks at the window. There is no sign of the GIRL. Near the front door there is a horse and a carriage, and a FOOTMAN brushing the horse.

Int the GIRL'S *bedroom – same day*

She is sleeping on the bed and we can see that she is ill. A DOCTOR is with her, and her PARENTS are standing near the bed. She stretches her hand to her MOTHER who holds it. She smiles and dies peacefully. Her MOTHER is weeping and the DOCTOR shrugs his shoulders in a gesture of hopelessness.

Ext the mansion – same day

The DOCTOR walks out of the mansion, and gets into the carriage. The NURSEMAID runs to the carriage and talks briefly with the DOCTOR. She goes away wailing, her hands on her head, as the DOCTOR rides away. The OLD MAN goes to talk with the FOOTMAN.

CU – OLD MAN

His eyes are glassy with unshed tears.

Ext the small town – the next day

The OLD MAN pushes his wheelbarrow on which there is his stereo set. He is walking confusedly on the street. A car screeches near him. It nearly knocks him down. The angry driver brandishes his fist at him and drives away furiously.

Follow OLD MAN

He gets to a building with the sign **PAWNSHOP**. He pushes the wheelbarrow into the building.

Ext the mansion – the same day

The funeral procession walks out of the mansion led by a priest followed by altar and choir boys. Other people are loading a small coffin into a horse carriage. All are wearing dark Victorian mourning costumes.

Ext the pawnshop – same day

The OLD MAN walks out of the pawnshop without the stereo or the wheelbarrow.

Follow OLD MAN

He crosses the street to another shop with the sign **TUXEDOS – FOR SALE OR HIRE**. He walks into the shop.

Int the tuxedo shop – same day

The old man is being fitted with a tuxedo.

Ext the cemetery – same day

There are well-tended graves all around. The girl's PARENTS, some RELATIVES and FRIENDS are standing in front of the small coffin. The CHOIRBOYS are singing a hymn in their angelic voices and the PRIEST has opened his book, ready to say the last rites. The OLD MAN, wearing his new tuxedo, comes running among the graves, and joins the crowd of mourners. They look at him uneasily. He steps forward and starts dancing to the rhythm of the hymn. There is consternation in the crowd, and the PRIEST signals to the choir to stop singing. There is complete silence, but the OLD MAN continues his waltz, gracefully holding his imaginary little partner.

CU – OLD MAN

There is ecstacy in his face as he dances to the absolute silence.

Include the crowd

Their consternation has turned into placid disbelief. The OLD MAN dances on, doing different variations of the dance.

Dissolve to:
Int the ballroom – the evening of the ball

The OLD MAN is dancing with the LITTLE GIRL, and the horrified crowd is looking on from the sides.

Dissolve to:
Ext the cemetery – day

The OLD MAN continues his dance, expertly executed, after which he takes a bow. The crowd does not respond.

Closer angle – the OLD MAN

He takes another bow. There is an outburst of applause.

Include the crowd

They are all applauding, albeit with placid, almost stone cold faces. They applaud for a long long time.

Fade out

BANNED

A play for radio

Characters

CYNTHIA

BRA ZET

POLICE OFFICER

MRS VAN WYK & WOMAN

BOY

GIRL

FIRST CHILD

SECOND CHILD

Banned was first broadcast by the BBC African Theatre on 28 November 1982. Cynthia was played by Elizabeth Adare and Bra Zet by Olu Jacobs. Sean Barret was the Police Officer, Elaine Loudon Mrs Van Wyk and Woman, Christopher Asante the Boy, Daphne Maurice-Jones the Girl, with Vicky Ireland as the First Child and Bernadette Windsor the Second Child. The production was produced and directed by Nick Barker

Scene One

SFX: Sound of jazz piano melody. After opening bars, CYNTHIA *hums an accompaniment. Piano fades out leaving* CYNTHIA *humming on her own.*

CYNTHIA: Good enough to fill any mother's heart with joy.
[*Pause*]

> I mean the bootees, not the song. The bootees I spend my days crocheting . . . that are lying around here . . . all over the room. The bootees. Mountains of baby bootees to keep the little feet warm and fill the mothers' hearts with joy.

[*Pause*]

> On the subject of mothers, we can do without them, don't you think? I mean, they are quite dispensable. Let's face this squarely, without bringing any unnecessary emotions into it. Mothers can be done away with, and I am talking from experience. I never had one. Of course somebody did give birth to me, but I never got to know her. She went to bring up other folks' children in the white suburbs of Johannesburg, whilst I grew up motherless in the townships. Nothing unusual. I spent all my childhood living with different people who were called aunts, grandmothers and what-have-you. And I managed without a mother, like a thousand others . . .

[*She laughs. It is a hollow laugh – almost as if she is mocking herself*]

[*Pause*]

I wonder what brings him back to mind. I mean, it was long ago. Bra Zet was one of my first cases after I'd joined a welfare society for disabled persons as a young, energetic, committed social worker.

He was born a welfare case, destined to die one. Bra Zet . . . I used to read about him in *Post*. Remember the *Golden City Post*? What a newspaper! Sex, rape, murder, armed robbery, divorce scandals, extortions . . . Wholesome reading for the whole family.

Bra Zet was a big noise in the gangster circles. At the time I did not know I would have close encounters with him.

He was the terror of the townships. Used to pull real big jobs. He and his gang. I forget what it was called now, but it was none of your small time gangs that pinch pennies from little girls sent to the corner store by their grandmothers.

Then one day it happened. Gang warfare broke out. And he was shot right on the spinal cord, paralysed from the waist down. That's how he became one of my cases. It was my job to counsel cripples.

Scene Two

SFX: Sound of piano being played on record player

BOY: Heita Bra Zet!

BRA ZET: Heita sonnyboy!

GIRL: Heita Bra Zet!

BRA ZET: Heita sweetie-pie! Hoezit?

GIRL: Sweet.

BOY: We have brought you the stuff. And this, I promise you, is the best that you can get. Die beste!

BRA ZET: Good, sonnyboy. Roll us a nice big zol. A nice big one, and we are going to smoke until we are stoned dead.

BOY: Okay Bra Zet.

BRA ZET: When are they coming . . . the other boys and girls?

GIRL: They will be here soon, Bra Zet. And they will be bringing more stuff and drinks.

SFX: BRA ZET puffs a cigarette, and sighs with pleasure

BRA ZET: Ja . . . This is great stuff, sonny . . . Great stuff!

GIRL: Ja . . . You deserve the best, Bra Zet. You are the greatest.

BRA ZET [*laughing*]: Even though I am now a cripple?

BOY: Nothing can destroy you, Bra Zet.

You are still the greatest!

They thought they could destroy you when they shot you, but they don't know what's coming to them.

[BRA ZET *laughs with pleasure*]

You are still going to lead your gang again, Eh, Bra Zet?

You are still going to pull the big jobs!

You are still going to . . .

I remember the days when you used to be the king of all the gangs.

I know those days are not over . . .

Joint laughter

Fade

CYNTHIA: Yes, they used to shower him with praises about his exploits in days gone by. Smoking zol after zol of dagga, those boys and girls, and showering him with praises. I could tell it was not mere flattery. Those boys and girls believed in Bra Zet.

I mean, he was a legend, and legends don't just die without even a whimper of a struggle.

[*Sighing as if still lost in thought*]

Ja . . . Now what about my crocheting.

Where's that new ball of wool?

Pause

Scene Three

SFX: A distant church bell rings and after a few tolls, stops. There is a knock off mic, which is immediately followed by the sound of the door opening. Voices of excited little children.

FIRST CHILD: We have come to play with Thandi.

CYNTHIA: She can't come out now.

SECOND CHILD: Why can't she come out now?

CYNTHIA: Go and play out in the street. She will come and play with you when she finishes washing the dishes.

SECOND CHILD: Awu, it's cold outside. We want to wait for her here.

CYNTHIA: No! Go out. It is the law that you can't be here.

FIRST CHILD: Why did you make that law?

CYNTHIA: I did not make that law.

SECOND CHILD: Who made that law?

CYNTHIA: The government . . .

SECOND CHILD: But this is your house!

CYNTHIA: Of course this is my house.

FIRST CHILD: Then why did the government make the law?

CYNTHIA: I . . . I don't know.

SECOND CHILD: Why don't you know?

CYNTHIA: Now listen, I don't have time to answer your questions. Please go.

[*Pause, then she shouts*]

Out! Out, I say! And don't come back!

SFX: Children running away. The door bangs after them.

My God! They couldn't understand. I hated doing that. I hated it!

[*She lets out a long sigh*]

Anyway let me go back to my crocheting.

[*Speaking in baby language*]

Now which nice baby is going to get these little bootees?

[*She chuckles to herself*]

I remember, I was telling you of Bra Zet.

I used to go to his dingy room. If you have been to Alexandra Township you have seen the kind of house I am talking about – long dark corridor with rooms opening upon it. Huge families living in each room. Dirty little children with dry tears down the cheeks, peeking at each other as unsteady footsteps are heard coming along. Babies crying. Mothers screaming at them to shut up. The stench of beer and urine. That's the kind of passageway I used to walk twice a week, sometimes slipping on baby shit or drunken man's vomit, as I fearfully moved on to counsel him. His small room was at the end of the tunnel, and it was always dark, with yellowing newspapers plastered on the only window.

Scene Four

SFX: Sound of piano music being played on record player, GIRL *and* BOY *talking and laughing in the background. There is a knock.*

BRA ZET [*as if in a stupor*]: Go away! Nobody wants you here!

SFX: Door opens

CYNTHIA [*coming on mic*]: Good afternoon Bra Zet.

BRA ZET [*mock joy*]: Oh, it's you my saviour. The great lady from Cripple Care Society! The beautiful Cynthia! [*Then angrily*] And where the hell is my motorised wheelchair?

[*Silence*]

Have you lost your tongue?

CYNTHIA: Would you mind turning that music down.

[BOY *and* GIRL *giggle*]

[*SFX: Music is turned down low*]

I have told you a number of times that Cripple Care will not give you a motorised wheelchair unless . . .

BRA ZET: Now you listen here, my girl. And listen proper, jy verstaan? Go and tell those white bosses of yours that if I don't get that wheelchair . . .

CYNTHIA: Why don't you take one of the jobs the society found for you? Do something that will earn you some money. Then you will get your motorised wheelchair. Those are the rules of Cripple Care, and I don't make them.

BRA ZET [*laughs mockingly*]: Look at me proper, my girl. Do I look like anybody who allows the likes of you to push me around? Ek is ou Bra Zet ek, jy verstaan?

CYNTHIA: I am just telling you what the policy of Cripple Care is.

BRA ZET: I don't give a damn about stupid policies. All I want is a motorised wheelchair. How the hell do you expect me to lead a normal life without a motorised wheelchair? What kind of a welfare society are you supposed to be anyway if you can't afford to buy me a motorised wheelchair?

CYNTHIA: Is there anything else I can do for you?

BRA ZET: Yes! Get lost.

[*SFX: Music is turned up very loud*]

And don't come back unless you are bringing me my motorised wheelchair.

CYNTHIA [*Going off mic*]: Well, goodbye. I'll see you again next week.

SFX: door opens and closes.

BRA ZET [*Shouting*]: Voetsek!

BOY *and* GIRL *laugh*

BOY [*Still laughing*]: Bra Zet, you shouldn't talk so rough to a beautiful lady like that. You are going to scare her from coming here to brighten our lives.

BRA ZET: Beautiful lady? What do you know of beautiful ladies? Jy is net 'n lighty. I have known models and beauty queens, man. Miss Johannesburg. Miss Soweto. You name them boy, they have passed through my hands.

[*A short pause*]

Scene Five

CYNTHIA: I dreaded the days I had to go to Alexandra Township to counsel him. I desperately wanted to pull out of that case. Couldn't stand that man. That whole place made me sick. I went to the boss to plead with her to transfer me to some other area . . .

The boss.

[*She laughs sarcastically as she remembers the boss*]

She was a no-nonsense Afrikaner lady. Matronly, but well-groomed. She relished sending chills of fear through the spines of all the social workers whenever she was around.

[*Pause*]

Mrs Van Wyk, I am sorry . . .

MRS VAN WYK: You don't have to be sorry, my dear. Just tell me what I can do for you. But first of all, is it very important?

CYNTHIA: I think it is.

MRS VAN WYK: You think, eh?

CYNTHIA: What I mean is, ma'am . . .

MRS VAN WYK: Never mind what you mean, my dear. I am more interested in what you say. Is it so important that the supervisors cannot deal with it?

CYNTHIA: Mrs Van Wyk, it is about . . .

MRS VAN WYK: And is it so important that it can't wait? You don't have an appointment, remember. Supposing I was having an important meeting.

CYNTHIA: Well, your secretary . . .

MRS VAN WYK: She did, eh? We'll see about that. What is your problem, my dear?

CYNTHIA: It's about the Alexandra Township case. The gangster who got paralysed in a gun fight. I have the file with me here.

MRS VAN WYK: Never mind the file. What is your problem?

CYNTHIA: Can you allow me to pull out of the case? You could put someone in my place. Maybe one of the male social workers. It frustates me that for all the months I have been counselling him I have not made any progress. He simply won't respond.

MRS VAN WYK: You never fail to amaze me. Are you trying to tell me that you are incompetent?

CYNTHIA: I am not incompetent! That man has threatened me with violence if I don't get him a motorised wheelchair.

MRS VAN WYK: Now, my dear, I want you to listen very carefully. You are going to work in Alexandra Township. And there you are going to deal with all the cases in our files. You are going to state clearly the policy of the so- ciety to your clients; namely, no unproductive cripple gets a motorised wheelchair. There is no exception to that rule. You will counsel that man until he takes a job. And I want to see results, my dear. I will give you a month to show me results. Now go back to your work, and let us hear no more nonsense about this.

Scene Six

CYNTHIA: My little girl, she can't understand why everything has changed. Why her little friends are not allowed to play with her at home any more ... Why I sit here at home all day long crocheting babies bootees. I have tried to explain to her, but how can she understand? How can anyone understand?

Last week her school presented a play and she was in it. But I was not there to share in her proudest moment. She couldn't understand why. Other mothers were there. I used to go with her to her school concerts. I used to accompany her to her friends' homes to attend their birthday parties. I used to take her to the cinema, or to visit grandma in Orlando East. Now I can't do that any more.

[*Pause*]

Because the law won't allow it.

Next week she will be celebrating her ninth birthday. She says she would like to have a party and invite all her friends. How do I tell her that a party in this house would be a risky business? I could end in jail.

All her friends have their parties at their own homes. I'll have to think of something. Maybe hold the party at a neighbour's house. And of course I can't be there myself to see her blow out her nine candles and make a wish. The law, you know. How can anyone understand?

The day after the battle with Mrs Van Wyk, I was late at work. There was excitement when I got into the office.

WOMAN: Cynthia, the boss wants to see you.

CYNTHIA: A few minutes late and the boss wants to see me?

WOMAN: Not about that. Something happened. And she looks real mad. Better go into her office at once.

SFX: A knock

MRS VAN WYK: Come in!

SFX: Footsteps coming on mic

MRS VAN WYK: Well, what do you have to say for yourself?

CYNTHIA: Nothing.

MRS VAN WYK: Nothing, eh? A man almost kills himself, and you say nothing.

CYNTHIA: Mrs Van Wyk, I don't know what you are talking about.

MRS VAN WYK: Was it not only yesterday that you were telling me you were not going to handle a certain Alexandra Township case?

CYNTHIA: I merely requested you to transfer me to some other area. You said no and that was the end of it.

MRS VAN WYK: That was not the end of it, my dear. Your client is in hospital after a suicide attempt.

CYNTHIA: Suicide! Oh, dammit!

MRS VAN WYK: What's that you said?

CYNTHIA: Oh, never mind.

MRS VAN WYK: Profane too, eh. Some upbringing. Now tell me, you had an argument with the client, right?

CYNTHIA: That's not true!

MRS VAN WYK: You said he threatened you. How did he come to threaten you?

CYNTHIA: I told you yesterday that he wants a motorised wheelchair, and . . .

MRS VAN WYK: Don't you think you failed somehow in handling this case?

CYNTHIA: What should I have done? What could I have done, Mrs Van Wyk?

MRS VAN WYK: Basic principles, my dear. Basic principles. This is not a school of social work. I expect all the employees to be versed with basic principles.

CYNTHIA: Mrs Van Wyk, do you really think any social worker could have stopped Bra Zet from cutting his throat if he wanted to?

MRS VAN WYK: I am not going to answer your impertinent questions. What I need from you is a full report on this case. You might have to appear before the board. And if that happens, my dear, God help you.

CYNTHIA [*almost screaming*]: I ought to be getting support from you! Instead you . . . you . . .

MRS VAN WYK: Will you please go out of my office?

SFX: Footsteps moving off mic. Door opened and banged shut.

Scene Seven

CYNTHIA: I pieced the whole thing together later.

Bra Zet had been smoking and drinking as usual, with his gang of hero-worshippers. One of the girls teased him about not being as brave as he used to be. He took a knife and slashed his knees. Blood oozed out and he laughed as the gang stood there horrified. He was rushed to hospital in an ambulance, laughing all the way.

Bra Zet had dangerous impulses. Always had. He was feeling that he was somewhat losing his grip on the gang, and he wanted to demonstrate to them that he was still the old Bra Zet, with all his bravery intact. If he can't impress them by moving around in style in a motorised wheelchair, he will impress them by showing how brave he is. How could they know that because of his paralysis he felt no pain?

I went to Baragwanath Hospital to see him.

The doctors told me it would be impossible for his wounds to heal. They would have to amputate both his legs. He refused. But as the days went on his wounds began to rot. The doctors had to amputate without his permission. He was discharged from hospital and I resumed 'caseworking' him. He was now a changed man, except for one thing. He still wanted his motorised wheelchair.

But he was no longer the abrupt self-assured Bra Zet who used to threaten me. He was a scared man, and dreaded meeting people – even his gang of youths. He thought the whole world was laughing at him. He spent all the time alone in his room, brooding. But at last he was beginning to respond to my counselling and I found myself spending hours with him, talking about everything under the sun. And I don't know when it happened. But suddenly he was something more than just 'a case' – a human being.

You know, Bra Zet was not my only client at the welfare for the disabled. I had hundreds of others. Old men. Women. Children. Oh, children. Young boys and girls; cut down, as the saying goes, in the prime of their youth. Cut down by bullets, paralysed for ever. Casualties of the June '76 riots.

Riots? They call them riots! Calling a people's struggle for freedom a riot! You will remember that many died. Others were crippled and became my clients. I saw them all – those in my area – counselled them, got them whatever assistance I could from the welfare society.

Of course this was an open invitation to the police. From time to time I was dragged to the police station for interrogation.

Scene Eight

POLICE OFFICER: Will you have tea?

CYNTHIA: Yes, thanks.

POLICE OFFICER: Most of the cripples you work with are the school children who were trying to rise against the government in 1976.

[*Silence*]

More tea?

CYNTHIA: No thanks.

POLICE OFFICER: I am sure you will want to help us in our investigations. Those children talk with you, right? About themselves . . . their families . . . their friends . . .

CYNTHIA: Sometimes. Yes.

POLICE OFFICER: And about their mates who are planning to . . . as they say, skip the country to join the terrorists.

CYNTHIA: Even if they had such information they wouldn't discuss it with me.

POLICE OFFICER: You know that there are many of these children who have escaped to neighbouring countries to join the terrorists?

CYNTHIA: All I know is what I read in newspapers.

POLICE OFFICER [*cynically*]: I believe you, eh . . . Cynthia. I believe you. And of course when you have . . . eh, information you'll let us know.

So long. I am sure we'll meet again soon.

CYNTHIA: At first I was intimidated. But when I became a regular guest of the interrogation chambers I became defiant. They got nasty. I became more defiant. [*She shouts, and her voice reverberates over and over until fade out*] Damn fools! Leave me alone! Let go of me! I am a social worker! I am only doing my job!

Scene Nine

CYNTHIA: You know, when you apply the basic social work principles in this country you run against the law. I don't care what agency you work for, you run against the law. It can be child welfare, or rehabilitation of criminal offenders. You run against the law. I learnt that the hard way. But I wasn't going to be bitter about it. Also I wasn't going to be a mere functionary like some social workers I know. I decided that the best thing for me would be to resign from Cripple Care. Do something constructive outside the establishment that stifled me.

At the same time I was so proud of my work. Oh, I was so proud of my work. Bra Zet was turning out well. He was responding to my counselling. He could now go out, meet people. There was even talk of getting him a job at one of the factories in the city. But I had to leave all that behind me. Others would take over and do just as good a job.

[*She hums the piano melody*]

[*Brief silence*]

SFX: There is a loud knock off mic

I wonder who that is.

SFX: Her footsteps going off mic. Door opens.

Bongie! Is it really you? Why, I never thought you'd come. I mean since I got banned and placed under house arrest I never heard from you. And we were such good friends at Cripple Care. Did everything together. Covered for each other. Lied for each other. Everything, Bongie. Like sisters. Yet you didn't come.

You know, I sat waiting for days and days. It's a lonely world, Bongie. Was it fear perhaps? Fear that the security police would come knocking at your door if you'd been with a banned person? Answer me Bongie. Was it fear? And the others we used to go to stokvels and soccer matches together, are they afraid too?

[*She laughs derisively*] You have lost your tongue. But let me tell you, the people have not lost their tongue. They have no fear any more. They have . . .

SFX: Footsteps of someone running away

No, don't run away, Bongie! I haven't finished yet. Listen to me, for your sake, before it's too late. Don't run away! I am a fighter, Bongie! I am a fighter! [*Shouting at Bongie who must now be very far*] I am . . . a . . . fighter!

Let the bitch go. [*Softly*] I am a fighter.

Yeah, after leaving the welfare society, for some time I didn't quite know what to do. I knew that I wanted to do something constructive for my people, but didn't know how to go about it. Didn't know what, in fact.

Then I heard of a group of community workers who were helping the squatters. Of course you know about the squatters. You have seen their shelters of plastic and cardboard. You have seen bulldozers flattening these shelters, and you have seen them rise again like a phoenix in a matter of minutes. You have seen those women and children, determined to live together as families, stand up in defiance of the police and government officials who are eager to send them to their so-called homelands.

I joined the community workers and we tried to help the squatters in various ways, such as collecting donations of blankets, firewood, food and clothing from those of us who were better off. Indeed people's hearts were touched when they learnt of mothers and their babies, out in the freezing cold and rain, having makeshift plastic shelters destroyed and the plastic confiscated by officials.

We went to the squatter camps, dispensing mugs of hot soup to the women and children. Children. Some living alone.

Scene Ten

SFX: Sound of wind and rain. Noise of women and children talking. Some laughing. Clatter of mugs and tins. Sound of liquid being poured into a tin container.

CYNTHIA: What is your name, sonny?

LITTLE BOY: Adam.

CYNTHIA: Where is your mother?

LITTLE BOY [*Tearfully*]: She is in prison.

WHITE WOMAN: Adam lives all alone. Sleeps wherever he can find shelter.

CYNTHIA: What happened?

LITTLE BOY: They came . . . the police . . . and took her away.

WHITE WOMAN: I took him home with me. But yesterday I had to return him to the squatter camp because I feared retaliation by the authorities for keeping an illegal black child in a white area. I have given him clothes and food, but I don't want any more trouble. Reprisals against my children . . .

SFX: Distant sirens off mic and fade out.

Scene Eleven

CYNTHIA: Sometimes police vans would come whilst we were helping the squatters, and all the black community workers would be arrested. The white ones would be sent home, or be fined for being in there without a permit. We would be interrogated for hours on end, then warned never to go to the squatter camp again.

But we went. We went.

My disillusionment increased as our arrests got regular. What were we doing, eh? I mean, we were giving temporary relief to a few squatters, but was that really solving anything? A mug of soup will sustain the spirit for a day, but will it change anything? Some decided to work directly with the squatters, to organise them into a mass movement that would launch an open defiance campaign.

Then one day they came. My daughter and I were getting ready to go to church that Sunday morning. Special delivery by three security police. A very special document from the Minister of the Interior. Eight pages of perverse instructions. I was banned, and my banning order was to include house arrest.

Thank you very much for the nice letter from your nice Minister. Now if you will excuse me. I have to go to church.

POLICE OFFICER: No, you can't go to church. If you read that 'nice letter' you will note that it prohibits you from leaving your premises at weekends.

CYNTHIA: What the hell! Your Minister of Interior prohibits me from praying to my God in my own way?

POLICE OFFICER: Not only that, Madam. It is illegal for you to meet more than one person at any one time. It's right there in black and white in the banning order.

CYNTHIA: You mean I can't go to work any more? How the hell do you expect me to live, and my little girl too?

POLICE OFFICER: You only have yourself to blame. If you hadn't gone on with your terrorist activities . . . And we warned you, you know. You can't say we have not been fair with you. Anyway if you want to take a job you have to apply for special permission, and I can't guarantee that the Minister will grant you one.

CYNTHIA: What the hell!

POLICE OFFICER: And note, madam, the banning order prohibits you from entering the premises of any factory and any institution of learning. Also you must be indoors between six pm and six am. You are not to be visited at home, and shall not go out at all on weekends and public holidays.

CYNTHIA [*shouting vehemently, her voice reverberating*]: Julle moer ma-an! No one of you has the right to deprive me of my freedom!

Scene Twelve

The following monologue is dreamlike . . . almost delirious.
SFX: footsteps and pattering coming on and off mic. She must
be busy going up and down.

CYNTHIA: What the hell! Who is free here? Nobody is free
here . . .

Just a minute. I am going out. I have a date. When
he comes we'll drive to Jabulani Amphitheatre. Then . . .
what? Ok . . . What dress am I going to wear? This red
one. Ja, I like this red one.

We'll go to Orlando Stadium to watch Pirates thrash
Kaiser Chiefs. He'll root for Chiefs and I'll root for Pirates. Then we'll quarrel . . . No, please no quarrels tonight.

Where is my cosmetic case? I have got to put on my
best make-up. And my jewellery box.

We'll quarrel and I'll leave in a huff. Take a taxi home.
He'll come and apologize profusely. Then we'll start the
evening afresh.

Let's see . . . Where shall we go next? I know where
we shall go . . . We'll go to Kolokoti's Shebeen. Sit there
and have a cold beer. Listen to jazz. The Bird. Coletrane.
Kippie Moeketsi. Malombo. Dolphy . . .

That's a perfect make-up that I have. Now let me see
what hairstyle I am going to make. OK I know what I
am going to do.

[*She hums the song of the piano. The original piano melody then accompanies her.*]

We'll stand up and dance . . . We'll go round . . . and round . . . like mad! And then we'll just sit down and listen. And talk . . . And laugh. Oh, how we shall laugh! Then I'll get drunk and demand to be taken home . . .

He'll make delaying tactics because he'll be enjoying the company of the other guys there – die anner blahs. I'll sulk. Then he'll drive me home . . . Then we'll make love . . . for the whole night. Oh, how we shall love!

Where is the mirror. Wow! Do I look beautiful!

[*She laughs deliriously for a long time*]
[*SFX: Cloth being ripped to pieces*]

Rip the stupid dress. Tear it to pieces. Dishevel the hair.

You know you can't go out. Rub the make-up off your stupid face. Rip the stupid dress to pieces! [*She resumes her normal tone*]

Well, you can get used to anything. I live my life the best way I can. It was lonely at first. Just me and my daughter. Of course neighbours are helpful. And my baby bootees . . . well somehow I manage to make ends meet.

Then one day I got a surprise visit.

Guess who . . . Bra Zet of course. He came driving his motorised wheelchair right up to my door. He was so changed, and that dazed look he always had was gone. He looked so handsome in his suit, so distinguished. But what was he doing visiting a banned person? Why take such a risk?

Scene Thirteen

CYNTHIA: Bra Zet! How did you find me?
What are you doing here?

BRA ZET: Why did you leave without even telling me?

CYNTHIA: But what are you doing here? We could both get into trouble!
Look Bra Zet, I had to leave. The welfare society was getting to be too much for me . . . And the police were harassing me every day.

BRA ZET: Ja. I hear you are a politician now. Read about you in the papers every day. That's how I found you. Been looking for you ever since. The welfare society refused to give me your address. But I kept on looking, man. Those newspaper blokes helped me too. Now I have found you. I found you Cynthia. . .

CYNTHIA: Bra Zet became my only visitor, every day.
A risk for both of us. We would sit together for hours. He would tell me stories of his days as a hoodlum. The things he used to do.
He would also proudly tell me of his job. He was a supervisor at a factory that manufactured cots, cribs and prams. He loved his job and was proud of the progress he had made. I would tell him of my life as a banned

person, a frequent guest of the state at John Vorster Square.

CYNTHIA: Bra Zet was often harassed by the police for visiting me. A number of times he was taken in for questioning. I pleaded with him to stop coming, but he would not hear of it. He loved me, he said, and visiting me was the least he could do for me. He hoped one day I would learn to love him too. [*She laughs*] Oh, well you know. . . It wouldn't have worked out, and you know why. He knew why too, and it made him look so pathetic.

Anyway he didn't bother about the police harassment. After all he had spent all his life in and out of the police station. In and out of jail. At least now he was being harassed for something legit, and that made him feel really proud. For once he was on the wrong side of the law for something which the people regarded as honourable.

About that time June sixteen was approaching, and there was talk throughout the townships of commemorating the June seventy-six resistance. There was talk of boycotting work that day and marching to John Vorster Square and demanding the release of all political prisoners.

June sixteen came. We were sitting with Bra Zet and my daughter in the living room . . .

I want you to know that I appreciate your coming here to see me every day since I got banned. You are a true friend.

BRA ZET: Actually it's for my own selfish reasons, Cynthia. I love you. You know it of course. And I want to be close to you. I keep hoping that one day . . .

CYNTHIA: There can't be a place for love in my life. My life is now committed to the struggle.

BRA ZET: Politics again! Politics! Goddamn politics!

CYNTHIA: I can't help it, Bra Zet. Look, I have something to tell you. . . I have decided to skip the country and join the fighters in exile.

BRA ZET [*shocked*]: What!

CYNTHIA: I am telling you this in confidence, Bra Zet. As a friend. So that you will not be surprised when one day you come here and do not find me.

BRA ZET: You are out of your mind, Cynthia! You are completely out of your mind! You have a daughter, Cynthia. Think of your daughter.

CYNTHIA: I'll take her home to my parents.

BRA ZET: Cynthia! Please, Cynthia!

SFX: Distant sound of school children singing and demonstrating

CYNTHIA: Listen. . . For the people to achieve liberation someone has to make the sacrifice, Bra Zet. Otherwise we wouldn't be having our soldiers fighting at the borders today, or infiltrating the country with arms.

I realize, Bra Zet, that peace has failed. We tried to change things through peaceful means. But somehow we have always ended behind bars, or banned or house arrested, or killed. In spite of our peace. That is why I have to go, Bra Zet.

BRA ZET [*almost hysterical*]: You can't do this to me, Cynthia I love you.

GIRL [*excitedly*]: Mama, the students are coming down our street singing.

STUDENTS [*singing*]: *Asikhathali noma siyaboshwa Sizimisel'inkululeko.*

SOME STUDENTS [*shouting in the midst of the song*]: Free Mandela! Release all political prisoners!

SFX: vehicles almost drown the song of the students and stop. The song of the students continues.

STUDENT: Police!

ANOTHER STUDENT: Police!

POLICE OFFICER [*speaking through a loudhailer*]: We warn
you to disperse peacefully and go back to your homes!
You have been warned.
Disperse! Disperse! Disperse immediately!

Song of the students continues

SFX: Gun shots

GIRL [*screaming*]: They are killing them, mama! They are
shooting the students.

SFX: Screams and sounds of people running in all directions

CYNTHIA: Oh, my God!
[*As a narrator*] Bra Zet suddenly drove his wheelchair
out of the door into the street screaming.

BRA ZET [*screaming*]: Not our children! You can't do this
to our children!

CYNTHIA: My God! They are going to shoot him down.
What shall I do! He's gone mad. They are going to kill
him. [*Nervous laughter*] He's heading straight for them!
[*Hysterical laughter*] A cripple charging the police in a
wheelchair! My God! Everybody is running away from
the cops, but Bra Zet is going straight for them. [*Moving
off mic she screams*] Come back, Bra Zet! Come back!

GIRL [*screaming*]: Ma-a-am! Come back! They will shoot
you!

SFX: Loud gun shot. Crazy laughter.

CYNTHIA: They shot him. [*Sighs sadly*] They shot him. I
saw his lifeless body sprawling on the bloody ground, his
motorised wheelchair upturned. Its wheels running round
and round. Running round like mad.

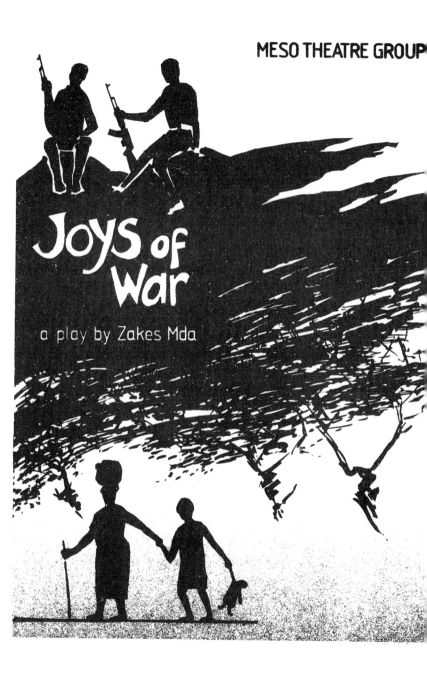

MESO THEATRE GROUP

Joys of War

a play by Zakes Mda

JOYS OF WAR

A play

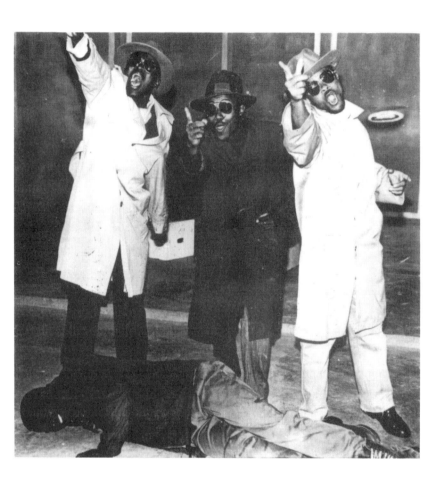

Characters

MAMA . . . . in her late fifties

NANA . . . . a girl of about twelve

SOLDIER ONE . . . . somewhere in his thirties

SOLDIER TWO . . . . more or less the same age

THE WOMAN

THE MAN

MOURNERS, INTERROGATORS, A WEDDING PARTY. . . these groups are composed of the same people. Any number will do.

Joys of War was first performed at the University of Zimbabwe, Harare on 26 August 1989 by Meso Theatre Group. Mama was played by Getrude Mothibe and Nana by Letlamoreng Mosenene. Francis Rangoajane was Soldier One and Kefuoe Molapo Soldier Two, with Maseabata Ramoeletsi as the Woman and Juda Monare the Man. Mourners, interrogators and the wedding train were played by Poloane Moroahae, Sehaole Mpopo, Thomas Monese, Juda Monare and Meseabata Ramoeletsi. The production was directed by Teresa Devant.

Act One

Scene One

The stage is divided into three acting areas which should be different platforms at varying levels so they are clearly distinguishable from one another. The levels do not only represent different places, but may sometimes represent different periods in the history of our characters. Lighting effects play a major role in enhancing the fine distinctions of time and space. Otherwise the stage is devoid of sets.

On the highest level sit two soldiers holding machine guns. They could easily be mistaken for silhouettes of statues in some war memorial. MAMA, *a worn-out woman in her late fifties enters at the lowest level. She is immediately followed by* NANA, *a tired girl of about twelve, carelessly dragging a rag doll. Both are carrying small parcels – presumably their provisions, for they are on a journey.*

MAMA: Nana, stop biting your nails. I tell you every day that it is bad manners for a young woman to bite her nails.

NANA: I don't want to be a young woman, Mama. I want to be a child.

MAMA: You cannot be a child. Not until we reach our destination. You were born a young woman, and you are going to remain a young woman – and behave like one – until we get there.

NANA: You promised we were going to rest after five miles.

MAMA: It's not five miles yet.

NANA: It says so right there on the signpost. Five miles.

MAMA: They intend for us to go from place to place.

NANA: Mama, I want to sit down and rest.

MAMA: Okay, but only for a few minutes. We must be elsewhere by dawn. They intend for us to wander.

NANA: When are we going back home, Mama?

MAMA: When we are done with wandering. Then we'll go back to help those we have left behind to rebuild from the ashes, as we have done in the past. Over and over again. Like the bird of old Egypt that your teacher taught you about at the school.

NANA: It's called a phoenix, Mama.

MAMA: Like the phoenix of old Egypt that lived for ever.

NANA: It lived for five hundred years.

MAMA: Only?

NANA: Then it built a big nest and set itself on fire. From the ashes a worm came out, from which the bird grew – young with beautiful red and gold feathers. In this way it lived for ever. Are we like the bird, Mama?

MAMA: Yes. Only we don't set ourselves on fire. They do it for us, but from the ashes we rise and grow.

NANA [*excitedly*]: With beautiful red and gold feathers!

MAMA: Gold yes, but red I doubt. Gold – maybe with black and green. Maybe like the little flags the people were waving when your papa led them against the raids . . . against the burnings.

You are biting your nails again Nana. You know I hate it when you bite your nails, you know that. Sometimes I think you just do it to infuriate me. And take out your

88

finger from your nostril. It's so obscene and not becoming of a young lady.

NANA: I told you I don't want to be a lady, Mama. I don't want to wander either. I want to go home. I want to play with my doll.

MAMA: At least it's alive this time.

NANA: But it's sick, Mama. Very sick. It was crying all night long. Couldn't sleep a wink.

MAMA [playing along]: Maybe it's hungry.

NANA: Every time I feed it it throws up. It's real sick, Mama.

MAMA: Did you take it to the clinic? Maybe the nurse will look at it, eh? Give it some injection. Soon it will be running around playing with the other children.

NANA: You know we don't have a clinic here, Mama.

MAMA: Yeah, I know that.

NANA: So why did you say I should take it to the clinic? You mocking me, are you Mama?

MAMA: I am not mocking. You take babies to the clinic when they are ill. Your mama took you to the clinic when you were a sick little baby. I took you sometimes when she was working in the kitchens.

NANA: But we don't have clinics here, you know that.

MAMA: Oh, yeah, you were always a troublesome one when you were a little one. Gave your mama and your papa a few sleepless nights.

MAMA slowly walks away, and sprawls herself a few feet from NANA.

NANA: I am sorry I gave you and my mother sleepless nights. But I am not sorry I gave papa sleepless nights.

MAMA: Child, you don't talk like that about your father.

NANA: Oh yeah? He makes us wander like this, eh, and sleep in the veld, and on top of that you want me to talk nice-

nice about him? Just because he's your son doesn't mean he's right, you know!

MAMA: One day you'll understand, Nana. Both of us will understand when we find the truth.

NANA: And look at my baby, she's going to die.

MAMA: She? Yesterday it was a he?

NANA: Of course it's a different baby, Mama. You know it's a different baby. Every day it's a different baby, until there won't be babies to die any more. And whose fault is that?

MAMA: Surely you don't blame your papa for that too?

NANA: For everything, Mama. He left, didn't he? When everyone needed him, he left us, and them, and everybody! He made promises, and then he left!

MAMA: We don't know for sure that he left, Nana. We are going to find out. That's why we are here.

NANA: I hate him! I hate him! I hate him!

MAMA: Girl, I won't sit here and listen to you talk dirty rubbish about your father.

NANA [*almost hysterical*]: And I hate you too! You are his mama, that's why you don't want to tell the truth about him! You know that he left! All the other children laugh at me because they say he ran away! When others were rebuilding he left! And we are not like the bird of old Egypt either! It's a lie! We are not like a phoenix!

MAMA *leaps at her, and shakes her violently*

MAMA: If you are going to behave like a spoilt brat I am going to shut your big mouth for you. You know very well that I know how to use a stick. You talk beyond your years too. I must get a piece of soap and wash your mouth . . . scrub your tongue.

90

NANA: Oh, Mama, I am sorry. It's because of my baby. She worries me so much since she won't get well. You know Mama I can't hate you no way. You are the gran'ma I have.

MAMA: And you better remember that.

NANA: I don't know what to do.

MAMA: Give her Epsom-salts. Small doses help if she's constipated. They'll clean her stomach, and soon she'll be running around the house.

NANA [*shocked*]: I thought she was asleep!

MAMA: What is the matter, Nana?

NANA: She didn't even cry!

MAMA: What are you talking about, girl?

NANA [*screaming and tearing the rag doll to pieces*]: Mama! She is dead! She died in her sleep!

MAMA *runs to her, and holds her in her arms. She is trying to comfort her. In the meantime lights dim on them and rise on the two* SOLDIERS. *We see their features for the first time.*

SOLDIER ONE: She died. You hear that? My little baby died. And all I could do was sit there and watch her die.

SOLDIER TWO: It is a sad story. But soldiers don't think about those things. All we have to think about is the war.

SOLDIER ONE: And you know what? We could have saved her. But they could do nothing, they said. We had no rights over that land, they said. We belonged to some barren place they designated us, they said. If they afforded us any facilities – even to save lives – we would be deceived into thinking that we belonged, that were there to stay, that they recognised our presence, that we were not squatters, they said.

MAMA *suddenly stands up and laughs aloud for a long time. The spot is on her, and the soldiers look at her in amazement.*

MAMA: Come child, it is time for our feet to talk with the road again.

NANA: You scared me, you know, with your haunting laughter. What was it all about?

MAMA: Sometimes we forget to laugh about these things. Then we remember when it's too late that we should have laughed, but we forgot.

MAMA *and* NANA *pick up their parcels and the pieces of the torn doll, and go out. The* SOLDIERS *resume their conversation.*

SOLDIER TWO: You always like to tell sad stories. If it's not dying babies, it's a prisoner hanging himself with a pair of jeans in a prison cell. I hate to listen to your sad stories.

SOLDIER ONE: Not hanging himself. They hang him, then tell the newspapers that he hung himself.

SOLDIER TWO: There you go again. Listen, I don't want to hear about your sentimental claptrap ... dying babies, hanging in the prison cell. I have a war to fight.

SOLDIER ONE: You have a war to fight. You are the only one who has a war to fight. You. You. You. What the hell do you think I am doing here? Spending a vacation?

SOLDIER TWO: Listen, mate, I didn't ask you to come with me here.

SOLDIER ONE: I didn't ask you to come with me either. But the fact is that we are both here now, and we've got to live with each other until our assignment has been completed. Only then can we go back to join the other cadres.

SOLDIER TWO: Am I looking forward to that! God knows how you have been getting into my nerves these past few days we have been waiting here.

SOLDIER ONE: You know, there is only one trouble with you.

SOLDIER TWO: What?

SOLDIER ONE: You are in love with yourself. You think you are the only thing that matters under the sun. You think you are the best thing that ever happened to this war. You think you are more committed to this war than all the other cadres put together.

SOLDIER TWO: I don't know why I should put up with all this nonsense you're telling me.

SOLDIER ONE: The Commander sent us on this mission together.

SOLDIER TWO: Special assignment.

SOLDIER ONE: On this special assignment together.

SOLDIER TWO: And we shall accomplish it even if I have to drag you to do it.

SOLDIER ONE: Who says you have to drag me? I am here, aren't I? The Commander didn't drag me from among the cadres. Like you I volunteered.

SOLDIER TWO: Then shut up and stop getting into my nerves.

SOLDIER ONE: You know, I didn't believe it when the other fellas said there was something wrong with you. You should hear the things they say behind your back. They think you are queer.

[SOLDIER TWO *glares at him.*]

No . . . not that kind of queer. They think you are strange. Not that I blame them for that. You don't let anyone get close to you, do you? Aloof. Don't want to make friends with anyone. All by yourself, in your own little island. You forget that war is team work. It's our war . . . all of us . . . because we believe in it. You are not going to turn it into private property.

SOLDIER TWO: There you go rambling again. God help me if I don't shoot you dead one of these days.

SOLDIER ONE: What did you say?

SOLDIER TWO: You heard me, pally. You heard me right. And I can do it, you know? I can do it, and tell the Commander some sad story about what happened to you. Can always invent a story.

SOLDIER ONE: You must be crazy . . . Of course you are joking, eh? You are serious then? I am sure you are joking. Ha! What a joke. It's a joke, isn't it? Just a joke?

Lights dim on the soldiers and rise on NANA *as she enters on the lowest level. She is lost. Spot follows her.*

NANA: Mama! Mama! Where are you, mama!

Lights rise on the soldiers as she exits.

SOLDIER ONE [*obviously trying to change the subject*]: Tell me, man, have you ever been in love?

SOLDIER TWO: Why you want to know?

SOLDIER ONE: Just curious. May explain something.

SOLDIER TWO: There was a woman . . . once.

SOLDIER ONE: I knew it! I knew it! I knew it!

SOLDIER TWO: She was very beautiful, and I thought I was going to marry her.

SOLDIER ONE: What happened?

SOLDIER TWO: I don't want to talk about it.

SOLDIER ONE: Maybe she died, eh, before you could get married? Maybe on your wedding day?

SOLDIER TWO: I don't want to talk about it.

SOLDIER ONE: Maybe she ran off with someone else.

SOLDIER TWO: I said I don't want to talk about it, dammit!

SOLDIER ONE: Maybe that's why you are so brave . . . always volunteering for the most dangerous assignments. You think you don't have anyone to live for any more. Now I understand.

94

SOLDIER TWO: You don't understand a damn thing. You jumping to your own conclusions.

SOLDIER ONE: I know deep down you are a nice human being . . . but she hurt you so bad you want to die.

SOLDIER TWO: You mean you volunteered because you want to die?

SOLDIER ONE: No! I have no intention of coming out of this war dead. I came to make a difference, not to die.

SOLDIER TWO: And of course you assume that some of us came to die.

SOLDIER ONE: Well, maybe I am wrong then. But I came . . .

SOLDIER TWO: Because your baby died?

SOLDIER ONE: You make it sound as though I am on a personal vendetta.

SOLDIER TWO: All I am saying is, we all have our different reasons. And who is to say what is personal and what is not?

SOLDIER ONE: There is no mysterious reason for my coming . . . for my joining in this war. To change things . . . to make a difference, as I said . . . to overthrow them and bring about a new system that will have regard for us working people. I tell you, man, any time of the day. At night even, while we slept . . . bulldozers would come and flatten our dwellings. Why? Because we are squatters in our own land. Soon as they left we would rummage among the heaps of debris and rebuild. Somebody must have suggested to them that fire would be a greater remedy and they came with gallons of petrol and set our dwellings on fire. But somehow we managed to rebuild. Again and again.

SOLDIER TWO: So you got tired of rebuilding.

SOLDIER ONE: I am sure they will continue to rebuild without me.

Enter NANA *at the lowest level. Although it is night at this level, the moon is quite bright. She is still looking for* MAMA.

NANA: Mama! Where are you?

MAMA *enters from a different direction.*

MAMA: There you are! What happened to you?

NANA: Oh, Mama, I am so scared! I got lost!

MAMA: You almost killed me with worry.

NANA: Whilst you slept I chased a butterfly.

MAMA: There are no butterflies at night.

NANA: I could have sworn it was a butterfly, Mama. It kept on enticing me by alighting on a blade of grass, and letting me get very close. But before I could catch it it flew away. It did that for a number of times, until I could not find my way back.

MAMA: That was a very foolish thing to do, Nana. You could have got lost for ever, and no one would have found you. Think of what your papa would say when he hears that you got yourself lost.

NANA: He doesn't care!

MAMA: Rubbish! Come let us sleep. We have a long journey in the morning. And don't you wake up and chase butterflies again.

They prepare to sleep on the ground.

SOLDIER ONE: They will never stop rebuilding, that I know. But we can't just go rebuilding, don't you think? We got to do something to stop the destruction permanently. I care for those people I left behind, and for my family, that's why I want to make a difference. You know, I have a little girl. About twelve or thirteen . . . I never can remember birthdays. My mama looks after her because her mama died at the birth of my second child . . . who also died.

MAMA *and* NANA *are now sleeping.*

SOLDIER TWO: There you go again! You don't ever get tired of talking, do you?

SOLDIER ONE: What about yourself . . . you didn't tell me why you came . . . I mean why you joined this war.

SOLDIER TWO: You know, I don't like to talk about myself. I am not like you. You know, you can go on and on talking about yourself. I like to keep myself private, you know. Doesn't mean that just because we are in the same war I got to reveal myself to everyone.

SOLDIER ONE: It does help though, to talk about things. Like now, you are morose, eh? Maybe because something is eating you, and you don't want to talk about it.

SOLDIER TWO: You know what I miss most?

SOLDIER ONE: Your family, perhaps?

SOLDIER TWO: Funerals.

SOLDIER ONE: Man, you *are* a strange one.

SOLDIER TWO: [*angry*] You wanted me talk about myself, didn't you? So now I am talking about myself and I am telling you that I miss funerals.

SOLDIER ONE: Okay, so you miss funerals. Don't get heated up about it, man. I always say a man has a right to miss anything he wants to miss.

SOLDIER TWO: [*showing a gleam of excitement for the first time*] Our funerals were social occasions. We gathered for the wakes, sang 'Nearer my God to Thee', and drank brandy smuggled in our jacket pockets. We dug the graves through the night whilst we joked about who was having an affair with who. In the course of it all some unfaithful husband would sneak away with someone else's mistress. The next day we buried the dead. In the midst of much weeping.

97

SOLDIER ONE: Somehow that doesn't sound nice.

SOLDIER TWO: So now you are going to moralise about it, eh?

SOLDIER ONE: I mean, I go to wakes too . . . but not the kind you are talking about. When you went to a wake . . . I mean there were different kinds of wakes. In some they sang, as you said 'Nearer My God . . .' or 'Peace, Perfect Peace' and the preacherman preached about the brotherhood of man and the fellowship of the Holy Ghost, and other things like that.

SOLDIER TWO: How were others different?

SOLDIER ONE: They did not seem to mourn for the dead. They raised their clenched fists and sang songs of freedom. They didn't have the kind of merriment you are talking about, but there was no weeping either. There was a lot of anger though.

SOLDIER TWO: Did it ever occur to you that deep inside they were crying?

SOLDIER ONE: I know for sure that they were angry inside. Very angry. I know because I was one of them and I felt the anger. I can still feel it now.

[*All of a sudden* SOLDIER ONE *is an angry speaker at a wake. As he speaks he is brandishing his machine gun. On the second level a group of mourners file in, softly singing a hymn. Their features cannot be seen for they have covered their heads with long black cloths. They solemnly sit on the floor. In the meantime* NANA *and* MAMA *have woken up, and are looking at the mourners. They both seem to be very frightened at this invasion of the past, and* MAMA *holds* NANA *tightly.*]

Oh yeah, brothers and sisters! We meet once again at a wake.

MOURNERS: Amen!

He descends to join the mourners at the second level where he will remain for the rest of this scene. The lighting here should be such that it will be associated with the hazy past, and is the same kind of lighting that will be used whenever the past is enacted.

SOLDIER ONE [*still brandishing his gun*]: Once again we gather to sing hymns and to vent our anger in songs and speeches. We do not mourn however, for our tears dried out long ago. We have seen the futility of weeping.

MOURNERS: Amen!

SOLDIER ONE: Today we gather to lament a young life, and to reinforce our resolve. Tomorrow some of us will take the trains and buses to the city, and to the industrial areas, and to the kitchens of the suburbs, to sell our labour, whilst others will march to the cemetery to bury the dead. Life will go on. Amen!

MOURNERS: Amen! Let it be!

He has finished his speech. NANA *is weeping uncontrollably and* MAMA *is trying to comfort her. The mourners stand up and each shakes hands with* SOLDIER ONE.

SOLDIER ONE: It's nice to see you again, sister.

MOURNER ONE: You look very well.

SOLDIER ONE: Thank you, brother. And how is the new baby?

MOURNER ONE: Not very well, I am afraid.

SOLDIER ONE: Hope he gets well.

MOURNER TWO: It was a good speech you gave.

SOLDIER ONE: I am glad you liked it.

MOURNER THREE: But it was very short, don't you think?

All of a sudden the mourners burst into a 'freedom song', clapping their hands and stamping their feet. From under their black mourning clothes they take flowers and throw them at him. These must be actual plastic flowers. At the lowest level the dim figures of MAMA *and* NANA *are angrily brandishing their clenched fists. The mourners go out still singing their song.*

SOLDIER ONE: What? Flowers! Plastic flowers! Flowers to weave a thousand wreaths! What on earth is happening here? [*Calling after the mourners*] Brothers and sisters, what with all these plastic flowers? You know what? Somebody wrote something like 'from bullets flowers shall bloom'. Yeah, I think it went like that. 'From bullets . . .' that's how it went. I can't say I remember who said it. But it looks like all that is left for us to say is 'from flowers bullets shall bloom'. From these plastic flowers bullets shall . . .

[*He pauses for a moment, and has a puzzled look*].

Do bullets bloom?

Sudden black.

Scene Two

Same as in previous scene. The two soldiers are once again like statues in a war memorial. MAMA *and* NANA *enter at the lowest level.*

NANA: Everywhere, they don't know where he is. We have been to interrogation centres, and to hospitals, and to mortuaries, and to . . . What are you going to do now?

MAMA: We are marching to the capital.

NANA: And when we get there?

MAMA: I am going to demand that they should set him free or bring him to trial. Then we shall all know what his crime is. Why are they afraid to let us know what he has done? Who do they think they are dealing with here? I am not a baby, you know. They can't tell me that they only took him for a day or two for interrogation.

NANA: They said they released him, Mama.

MAMA: That's what they say, but we know differently. We know they never let you go once they've got you. We saw them take him away, didn't we?

NANA: But you said . . .

MAMA: Okay, I didn't personally see them. But other people did. Those who were in the thick of the crowd with him when they threw the tear gas. They saw them take him away. Did we see them bring him back? If you did, I didn't.

Lights dim on MAMA *and* NANA, *and rise on the soldiers*

SOLDIER ONE: Anything could happen in those raids. It was exciting too, in its own sad way. There would be dogs charging at the protesters, or there would be tear gas thrown at them. All hell broke loose. Protesters would throw stones and would receive bullets in response. Sometimes bullets would start first, and protesters would throw stones in response.

SOLDIER TWO: You can't fight bullets with stones.

SOLDIER ONE: In the midst of it all, some would be burning the dwellings . . . the shelters we called home. Some of us would be picked up in our dazed state and loaded into pick-up vans to interrogation centres, others would go into hiding, perhaps hoping to surface when everything had cooled down.

Lights dim on the soldiers and rise on NANA *and* MAMA.

NANA: But others say they saw him run away. Then again they saw him at the bus stop with a luggage . . . running away on us.

MAMA: That is why we must find him, to show them that it is not true.

NANA: Mama, we went to all the interrogation centres and they say they don't know where he is.

MAMA: That is why we are marching to the capital. Come, come, girl. Let's walk on. We are not going to be resting after every few minutes. We are marching to the head-quarters where they have all the torture chambers, and we are going to demand his release. I am going to tell them to either release him or lock me up with him.

NANA: What about me?

MAMA: I guess if they lock me up they'll have to lock you up to.

NANA: I don't want to be locked up.

MAMA: No one wants to be locked up.

NANA: Then why are we doing this?

MAMA: For your papa.

NANA: My friends say . . .

MAMA: They listen to the gossip of their parents. You should know better than to believe the kind of rubbish they say.

NANA: How do you know he didn't run away, Mama?

MAMA: A mother always knows.

NANA: Mama, what's going to happen to my doll when we are locked up?

MAMA: They are going to lock you up with it.

NANA: But Mama, how am I going to bring up a baby in prison? You know how sickly he is.

MAMA: Thank God he is not dead this time. These past few days on the road I have had it up to here with dying babies. Your dolls always die.

NANA: He has lived so far because I took very good care of him. I took him to the clinic in the city and pretended I didn't come from the squatter camp. But he'll surely die in prison, Mama.

MAMA: You'll learn to cope. Women bring up their children in prison every day. Come, come, girl. Let's walk on. It's a long long way to the capital.

They go out. Lights slowly rise on the soldiers.

SOLDIER ONE: You know, I have been thinking about what you said. I don't like it one bit. I didn't join this war because my baby died.

SOLDIER TWO: And who said you did?

SOLDIER ONE: You said so. And I've been thinking about it a lot since you said it. I am not on a personal mission of vengeance. I am on a war of freedom. Long before my baby died I led the people against the raids. I led the working people against their masters. Long before my baby died.

SOLDIER TWO: Dying babies again, eh? You got to hammer on that, eh? You are obsessed with dying babies.

SOLDIER ONE: You know, when my baby died, her mother followed a few days after. And I was left a widower with a young daughter who had just started school. Thanks God I had my mama to look after her. Don't know what I would have done without her. Not everyone was as lucky. I mean, babies were dying every day. Especially when it was winter and the bulldozers came. Or when it was summer and there was no water for miles around. Or when . . .

SOLDIER TWO: Listen, mate, I know things have been tough for you. But the hell, things have been tough for everyone. You see all those cadres we left there? Every one of them has a problem, man. Well, their babies didn't die, maybe. Or they never lived in squatter camps like you. They come from cities and from farms and from every place you can imagine. But they all had problems. Every one of them has a story to tell. But you don't hear them boring everyone to death with sentimental nonsense. So shut up, for heaven's sake. Let's have some little peace.

SOLDIER ONE [*laughing*]: Both of us holding AK 47s. We are on a military assignment, and you want some little peace.

SOLDIER TWO: Between the shootings and the bombings we are going to have some little peace around here if I can help it.

SOLDIER ONE: Oh no, we are not going to have a little peace around here. We are not going to have a little peace anywhere in this country until we win this war.

SOLDIER TWO: Well, you go on making yourself a nuisance, and see if I won't soon have a little peace around here. You go on until something snaps in me.

SOLDIER ONE: You know what? I don't trust you. I don't feel safe with you here. After all you did threaten to kill me.

[SOLDIER TWO *ignores him, and rolls himself a cigarette*].

I don't think you can do it though. I mean, you might be strange and all that. But I don't think you are capable of murder.

SOLDIER TWO: Perhaps you have forgotten why we are here.

SOLDIER ONE: No! No! Not murder. We are soldiers fighting a war. When the sign comes we will detonate and destroy their munitions dump. Some of their soldiers who guard it will die. Perhaps some civilian passers-by too. That's how things happen in a war. It's not murder. But if you kill your own comrade-in-arms, well, it can't be anything but murder. And I would like to think that you are not capable of it.

[SOLDIER TWO *nonchalantly walks about, smoking his roughly rolled cigarette.*]

I mean, the way you carry yourself about, eh? Don't you think it makes me uneasy? You walking up and down like that, pretending to be important. Look, pally, I want you to know that I am not scared of you. I am not damn scared of you, do you hear that? You want to kill me, eh? Kill me then. Go ahead and kill me! Kill me and see what you are going to tell the Commander.

SOLDIER TWO: That you were a traitor. I shot you when you were running to warn them that we were going to detonate their dump.

SOLDIER ONE [*very scared*]: You are demented! you are . . .

SOLDIER TWO *runs back to him.*

SOLDIER TWO: I am sorry! I didn't mean that! I really didn't!

SOLDIER ONE: Man, you scared me, you know that?

SOLDIER TWO: It's all this pressure . . . waiting for the sign. My God, I hope it comes soon, so that we may be done with the job and go back to join the other cadres.

SOLDIER ONE [*relieved*]: So it was just a joke, eh?

SOLDIER TWO: Yeah, just a joke.

SOLDIER ONE: You know, I almost believed you. Almost. But deep down I knew that you were joking. I mean, you are one of the cadres, right? And you are the one who always goes for the most dangerous missions. Only last week the Commander was telling us that you were the best example of utmost dedication to the liberation struggle. Only last week, man. It would be very much unlike you to do a thing like that. Very much unlike you [*Laughs*] Wait till I tell the cadres of your impish sense of humour!

SOLDIER TWO: Listen, pally, let's just forget about it, eh? As far as we are concerned it never happened.

SOLDIER ONE: You know, they see you gloomy every time. They see you sombre. They don't know that deep down inside you have such a rich sense of humour. Almost scared me to death, eh? And you looked so serious. I would have sworn you were going to do it. Boy, you must have been an actor, man. I mean before the war and all that.

SOLDIER TWO: I would suggest that we keep this little joke between us two. No need to tell the cadres about it.

SOLDIER ONE: You must have been an actor, eh? Tell me honestly, man, you were an actor, eh?

SOLDIER TWO [*reluctantly*]: Er . . . sort of.

SOLDIER ONE: I knew it! And so modest too! You are an actor!

Lights down on the soldiers, and rise on the lowest level, as NANA *and* MAMA *enter. They are both very tired.*

MAMA: It was not a mistake. Couldn't be a mistake.

NANA: I got all the pieces here. Right here, all of them.

MAMA: Then you going to do it again?

NANA: Are you not going to help me then? You always so good with your hands.

MAMA: Okay, I'll help you. But I don't see what good it'll do.

They sit down to rest, and, with pieces of rag, make another doll for NANA.

MAMA: What I mean is, we making your doll again.

NANA: Yes.

MAMA: We make another one, yet we know that sooner or later it's going to die.

NANA: Is that not what always happens, Mama?

MAMA: Maybe you are right. Sooner or later they die, and we know that even when we make them.

NANA: My only worry is that I won't know what to do with her in prison.

MAMA: Don't you worry, little one. They may not lock us up, after all. All we want is to find your papa, and to find the truth.

NANA: Mama, if it's true that he is in prison like you say, I don't see why we should be taking this journey. He has

107

been in prison before, but we didn't take the journey to the interrogation centres of the capital.

MAMA: We knew where he was then, Nana. We knew he was in the local prison in town. They didn't let us see him, but we took him food and cigarettes. We took him clean clothes every other day. We knew he was there. They didn't deny that they had him either. And the lawyer told us he saw him.

Lights rise on the soldiers.

SOLDIER ONE: I was once an actor too, you know. When they held me at the local prison in our town, I was an actor.

SOLDIER TWO: You were an actor in prison?

SOLDIER ONE: That's right. In the prison cell with the other prisoners. In the interrogation chambers even.

SOLDIER TWO [*rather incredulous*]: An actor . . . at the interrogation centre?

SOLDIER ONE: Yeah, they held me for six months – incommunicado. Six months! Well, five incommunicado, since the first month they locked me up with petty criminals. You know, pickpockets and fellas who steal wheelbarrows and car batteries. Fellas who commit burglaries in the suburbs. Small time fellas, I say. I later heard from one warder that it was their way of humiliating me. I mean, political prisoners are always locked up alone, you know.

SOLDIER TWO: I don't know.

It seems as if SOLDIER TWO *has resigned himself to listening – at least for a while.*

SOLDIER ONE: Com'an, I am sure you know . . . I haven't met anyone who has not been to prison. Anyway when they locked me up with petty criminals, they thought the criminals would rough me up a little bit. They have a

108

reputation of roughing up new inmates, but it's all a lie. I didn't see them roughing anyone up. Those fellas welcome you, man, and make you feel at home immediately you are thrown into the cell. They ask you what you are in for and share their cigarettes with you. And stories of their crimes. And give you plenty of legal advice. And they knew about me too, you know? They didn't come from the squatter camp, but they knew about the raids there. And they were very angry about the whole matter. They came from the townships and from farms and villages, but they knew all about the squatter settlements. And the raids. And the burnings.

SOLDIER TWO: Of course they knew about the squatter settlements. Everyone knows about that. The whole country is a squatter camp. We are all squatters, that's what they have turned us into.

SOLDIER ONE: You know, I never thought of it that way. You are right, man. You are completely right. We are squatters in our own land. I guess that's why we are here waiting for the sign.

Lights rise on MAMA *and* NANA. *They have finished reconstructing the doll.*

MAMA: There now, it's done.

NANA: Ohh . . . and it's so beautiful, Mama. It's more beautiful than all the others.

She walks around singing a lullaby, then dances in excitement. MAMA *claps her hands in accompaniment. The soldiers look on with disinterest.* SOLDIER TWO *smiles briefly and cynically, then turns to* SOLDIER ONE.

SOLDIER TWO: So you were an actor once . . .

SOLDIER ONE: What? You interested in my stories now, eh? You actually want me to tell you one of my stories.

SOLDIER TWO: I have no choice. I am stuck here with you. Whether I like it or not you are bent on talking endlessly of your sentimental nonsense. I might as well choose which of the nonsenses I am going to listen to.

SOLDIER ONE: That's unkind of you to say that.

SOLDIER TWO: I didn't come here to be kind. The day I want to be kind I'll resign from the liberation army and go and set up an orphanage somewhere.

SOLDIER ONE: All right, don't you get angry now. You don't want to remind me of your joke now, do you?

SOLDIER TWO: What?

SOLDIER ONE: You don't want me to tell the cadres of your sense of humour, do you?

SOLDIER TWO: That's blackmail!

SOLDIER ONE *laughs.* MAMA *and* NANA *have finished their little ritual.*

NANA: She is so beautiful. I am not going to lose this one. Never, never!

MAMA: I hope not, Nana. I hope not. I don't like it when your dolls die. It's costing us too much time. We have to sit down and mourn, and then make another doll. In the meantime we don't know what they are doing to your papa.

NANA: What do they do to them in prison, Mama?

MAMA: They take them to interrogation chambers and torture them. Come, let's go, girl. We still have a long way to walk.

NANA: You know Mama, I still don't really really believe that they have him. I still think he ran away.

MAMA *and* NANA *go out.*

SOLDIER ONE: Those interrogation centres! They took me from the cell to the centre every day. Every day!

SOLDIER TWO: And what do they do there?

SOLDIER ONE: You mean you have never been to an interrogation centre?

SOLDIER TWO: I wouldn't be asking you, now, would I?

SOLDIER ONE: I mean it's very much unlike you that you have never been there.

SOLDIER TWO: Maybe I was much too smart for them.

SOLDIER ONE: They got eyes everywhere. They got ears too. Even amongst ourselves there are people who work for them. At the squatter camp we knew that sooner or later they were going to get all the information whenever we held our meetings. I don't understand how you got involved in politics but never got to see the inside of an interrogation chamber.

SOLDIER TWO: Like I say, I must have been too damned smart for them. Anyway, are you going to tell and finish the story or not?

SOLDIER ONE: You know, after a month, when they realized that I was getting on too well with the criminals, they took me to solitary. I mean it was too good to last in that prison cell with those fellas. We sang and told stories, and danced. That's where I became an actor. They used to help me rehearse the part I was going to play the next day in the interrogation chambers. That was the only way to escape the pain of torture. To act. And lie. And scream the way they want you to scream when the electric current ran through your body. We insulted them, and called them names, and rebelled against the warders. They realized their mistake and took me to solitary. And continued to take me to the interrogation chambers every day.

On the second level enter four INTERROGATORS. *They are parodies of the sinister spy or secret police of the old movies*

111

*– hats almost to the eyes, raincoats, and dark glasses. The
hazy lights of the past.*

SOLDIER ONE: See, they are there! The interrogators!

SOLDIER TWO: What?

SOLDIER ONE: The interrogators, man!

SOLDIER TWO: Man, you getting crazy, or what?

INTERROGATORS *are beckoning to* SOLDIER ONE *to join them.
At the same time they are softly humming an eerie song.*

SOLDIER ONE: I tell you, man, that's the same chamber too.
    The room with the big map on the wall. The room with
    the big map and red pins all over.

SOLDIER TWO: Well, why don't you go and face them, then?

SOLDIER ONE: No!

SOLDIER TWO *shoves him roughly and he tumbles down until
he lands in the midst of the* INTERROGATORS. *His gun has
fallen on the highest level and remains there.*

SOLDIER TWO: Go, dammit! Maybe one will be able to get
    some peace and quiet around here!

SOLDIER TWO *sits down, and becomes a war memorial statue
as the lights go down on him.*

INTERROGATOR ONE: You are going to tell us. Today you
    are going to talk.

INTERROGATOR TWO: Today you are going to talk. Sit down!
    Right there on the floor!

SOLDIER ONE *squats on the floor, where he will remain until
the interrogators leave.*

INTERROGATOR THREE: You are going to tell us everything
    you know.

INTERROGATOR FOUR: You are going to sing like a bird.

INTERROGATOR ONE: Sing like a bird!

SOLDIER ONE: I told you I have nothing to sing about!

112

INTERROGATORS *all stamp their feet and create a great clamour.*

INTERROGATORS: That is a lie! You are going to sing! You are going to tell us of all your terrorist activities!

SOLDIER ONE: I am no terrorist, I tell you. I lead a workers' movement. I lead the homeless squatters.

INTERROGATOR ONE: And who supports you, eh? Who gives you money for your movement? Who teaches you all the tactics of making riots and rebellions? How many people from your movement have gone to join the terrorists in the neighbouring countries? Sing, boy, sing!

SOLDIER ONE: Nobody teaches us. We are working people fighting for our rights. All we want is to own the product of our labour.

The INTERROGATORS *stamp their feet and shout again.*

INTERROGATORS: Terrorist! Communist! Liar! Terrorist! Liar! Terrorist! Liar! Terrorist!

SOLDIER ONE [*in the din*]: Help! Help!

INTERROGATOR TWO: We know all about you. Some of your people have confessed. So there is no use you getting obstinate here. We'll only release you when you have told us the truth.

SOLDIER ONE: But I told you, I have nothing to tell.

INTERROGATOR THREE: You'll soon have something to sing about. Wait till you get to the torture chambers, then you'll have something to tell.

INTERROGATOR FOUR: If all else fails we are going to throw you out of the window. You know what floor this is?

SOLDIER ONE [*scared*]: No.

INTERROGATOR THREE: Seventeenth floor.

SOLDIER ONE: You can't do that.

INTERROGATOR ONE: Who is to stop us?

INTERROGATOR TWO: We have done it before, you know. Thrown terrorists out of the window. We can always claim that you committed suicide.

INTERROGATOR FOUR: Show him the map first.

INTERROGATOR ONE: Yeah, you see the map on the wall?

He points at a wall that cannot be seen by the audience.

SOLDIER ONE: I have looked at it every day you take me to this interrogation chamber.

INTERROGATOR TWO: So you know what all those red pins are about?

INTERROGATOR ONE: He knows all right. Terrorist camps, that's what they are. All the terrorist camps in the neighbouring states. And the dates when such camps were established. And the strength of terrorists in each camp. It's all on that map. We know all their movement to infiltrate the country with arms to overthrow our lawful government. You must know something about that too otherwise you would not be creating riots all over the place. We know who you are, and you are going to confess everything today.

INTERROGATOR FOUR: Wait till you see today's special. We have re-equipped the torture chamber. State-of-the-art torture paraphernalia. Guaranteed to make you sing.

They laugh, and walk in line towards the exit.

INTERROGATORS: Come, boy, come! Come for your daily medicine! Or for the window!

SOLDIER ONE: No! No! I told you I don't know anything! No! You have tortured me every day. But I am not going to tell you anything more than I have done. Go ahead! Kill me! Throw me out of the window! You will only be destroying me. But sooner or later you will know that I am one of many!

The INTERROGATORS *have gone out, and all of a sudden* SOLDIER ONE *realises that he is alone. There is a glare of light. He looks around ashamedly. Spot follows as he runs to the highest level and lights rise on this level when he gets there, as the glare suddenly disappears.*

SOLDIER ONE: Why did you shove me, man? Why did you shove me?

SOLDIER TWO: You were speaking some gibberish I didn't understand.

SOLDIER ONE: That didn't give you the right to shove me like that.

SOLDIER TWO: Okay, I am sorry.

SOLDIER ONE: And I was not talking any gibberish. I was telling you of the interrogation centres and their torture chambers.

SOLDIER TWO: I don't know what came over me. I just felt the urge. The next thing I saw you rolling down the hill.

SOLDIER ONE: All right. But don't you do that again. It's going to make me believe your joke was serious after all. Remember the joke?

He picks up his gun and brushes the dust off it.

SOLDIER TWO: Are you ever going to forget that?

SOLDIER ONE: Not if you keep on reminding me.

SOLDIER TWO: I want to listen to your story, you know. Right up to the end. I am interested, really. So, there were interrogation chambers and big maps on the walls.

SOLDIER ONE: You know, when they ultimately released me I kept on thinking about the big map on the wall.

Enter MAMA *and* NANA *on the lowest level, continuing their journey.*

MAMA: I don't think prison agrees with your papa. He was never the same after they released him from the local prison. Always brooding.

NANA: And they took away his temper too, you know Mama?

SOLDIER ONE: I kept on thinking about the red pins.

SOLDIER TWO: What about them?

MAMA: He had too much on his mind, my poor boy. We all could see that.

SOLDIER ONE: I kept on thinking, maybe the red pins have the right idea, I mean the solution to our problems. I am going to join them, I kept on thinking. That's the only way I can remedy the situation. I am going to join the red pins on the map on the wall of the interrogation centre.

NANA: Maybe that's the time he was planning to desert us. Maybe that's what he was brooding about.

SOLDIER TWO: So that's how you came to join the cadres.

SOLDIER ONE: That's how I came. There was one of the many raids at our settlements.

MAMA: How many times will I tell you that he did not desert us. He was taken by the police during the raid.

SOLDIER ONE: And as usual they arrested me, together with all the people they call agitators. This time they only held me for a few hours and let me go. They are unpredictable, you know. They can hold you for years, for six months or for a few hours. It's all in the game they play with you. Just one of the ways they torture you . . . killing you with suspense, since you never know what they'll do next. Anyway when they set me free, I 'skipped the country', as they say, and went to join the cadres. And presto! Here I am, back in the country again on a special assignment of sabotage.

NANA: I know you told me, Mama. But I still don't believe that. I think when we get to the capital they are going to tell us the same thing that others have already told us – that they don't know where he is.

MAMA: Come, let's go, girl. The more I hear you talk this nonsense the more I want to prove to you that you are wrong about your papa. This time no resting after every three or four miles. We have to get to the capital.

MAMA *and* NANA *go out.*

SOLDIER TWO: You know, I think in many ways I misjudged you.

SOLDIER ONE: I am glad to hear you say that.

SOLDIER TWO: Maybe you talk too much, but you don't mean any harm. You are a soldier, a bit over-friendly, but you are a true soldier if ever I saw one.

SOLDIER ONE: Thanks, pally. I think I misjudged you too. I think I know you better than those other cadres do. They don't understand you, you know? But I have said it before, and I am saying it now, deep down inside you are a fine sensitive human being.

SOLDIER TWO: There you go spoiling it again . . . sensitive human being! Man, don't you understand that we are in a war?

SOLDIER ONE: Okay, I'll cut out 'sensitive' and just leave 'human being'. Phew! Never seen anyone who gets so mad when you try to say something nice about him. 'Sensitive', what does it matter? I for one am in this war because I *am* sensitive.

The sun is about to set and has filled the skies at the horizon with a pinkish-purplish colour.

SOLDIER TWO: Look, let's not start again . . . just when I am beginning to gain some little respect for you.

SOLDIER ONE [*very excited*]: For me! Respect for me!

They embrace, albeit with a little reluctance on the part of SOLDIER TWO. *Lights slowly go down on them, and for a while they become silhouettes of statues in a tight embrace against the setting sun. Lights black.*

Act Two

Scene One

SOLDIER ONE *has dismantled his automatic weapon and is cleaning its parts, while whistling, humming and singing to himself. After some time* SOLDIER TWO *enters on the second level jogging, and creeps, as though in a combat manoeuvre, to the highest level, where he startles* SOLDIER ONE.

SOLDIER ONE: What the hell!

SOLDIER TWO: It's only me.

SOLDIER ONE: Don't you ever do that to me, man!

SOLDIER TWO: What are you doing?

SOLDIER ONE: Cleaning my gun. Keeps me busy.

SOLDIER TWO: Are you crazy? This is no time to be cleaning your gun. You should always have your weapon ready for action.

SOLDIER ONE: Oh yeah? So now I can't even clean my weapon?

SOLDIER TWO: What if we are ambushed, eh? How are you going to return the fire? You just going to sit there and die with a clean gun?

SOLDIER ONE: Man, you like to be so particular about everything!

SOLDIER TWO: That's not a very smart thing to do, you should know that. What if the sign comes, eh? What if the sign comes and you are sitting here cleaning your gun? I don't like ineptitude in my men. We must always be in a state of alertness. Always.

SOLDIER ONE: I am not your man. You are not going to pull that rank stuff on me.

SOLDIER TWO: Who's talking of rank? We don't have ranks in this army, but you must admit that I am more experienced than you are in this sort of business. I have been on several such assignments. And you . . . This is your first, isn't it?

SOLDIER ONE: Yeah, it is my first, but . . .

SOLDIER TWO: So you must listen when I tell you. It's our lives you are playing with, you know? And if we are captured, or shot dead after all the planning that went into this . . .

SOLDIER ONE *puts his gun together.*

SOLDIER ONE: All because I cleaned my weapon!

SOLDIER TWO: Be as sarcastic as you want. Soon it's going to be time, and you are going to learn a bitter lesson, if you will be alive enough to learn.

SOLDIER ONE: I am not being sarcastic. I do understand what you are trying to tell me. There, I have put it together, see? Happy now?

SOLDIER TWO: Soon we are going to detonate.

SOLDIER ONE: Yeah.

SOLDIER TWO: And clouds of smoke and fire will go up, and buildings will come crumbling down. Screams and yells will be swallowed by the deafening music of the bombs.

SOLDIER ONE: You speak of it as if it's a festival of fireworks. There is some joy in it, as though we are talking of a game.

SOLDIER TWO: All wars are games. Like pieces of draughts on a board.

SOLDIER ONE: Only in wars lives are at stake. I don't like it when innocent civilians die.

SOLDIER TWO: Are you getting cold feet?

SOLDIER ONE: No . . . not at all. I am merely telling you my feelings about the civilians. I know that what I am doing is necessary, but I am not going to pretend that I enjoy it. If that is a weakness, then call me a weakling.

SOLDIER TWO: No, you are not a weakling. I told you I was gaining some respect for you, and I was damn right. Some of us killed those feelings long ago, even before we joined this war. It is not the war that killed them for us. I am the last one to look down on those who still have them.

SOLDIER ONE: Long before you joined the war? What killed them for you then?

SOLDIER TWO: Maybe one day I'll tell you. But as for now, let us concentrate on this assignment. Yeah, maybe one day I am going to tell you all about it. I've got to tell someone sooner or later, and you strike me as a sympathetic man.

SOLDIER ONE: You are making me curious now. You know, you have never told me why you joined this army. From what I notice, you were not very political in your civilian days.

SOLDIER TWO: I don't talk about that. It's all in the past.

[*There is a long uneasy pause.*]

You know, it is not the policy of our movement to kill innocent civilians.

SOLDIER ONE: Of course I know that. But they die anyway, don't they?

SOLDIER TWO: That happens, yeah, and it cannot be absolutely avoided. We don't go out of our way to kill civilian people, even from the enemy camp. You remember the well-publicised bombing of their air force building in the capital?

SOLDIER ONE: Yeah, I remember that. It was before I joined the army, but I remember vividly. The story was in all the papers.

SOLDIER TWO: And the papers highlighted the maimed and dead civilian passers-by, eh? Some of our people dead, or crippled. Now others asked, if these people are fighting for us, why do they kill us? They asked, and I tell you, they were right to ask that question. And of course the enemy played on that too. What I am trying to say to you is that we shall continue to fight this war, and destroy their munition dumps, and their power stations, and their buildings, and their soldiers together with their collaborators. In the process innocent civilians will die, and such questions will continue to be asked. This is something we all learn to live with. It cannot be avoided. It is painful, but it cannot be avoided.

SOLDIER ONE: You are right. You know what? Not only are you a brave soldier, but you are very wise too. I admire your wisdom. I think one day you'll be the commander of all our armed forces.

SOLDIER TWO: I have no such aspirations.

SOLDIER ONE: Honestly, man, I think you will make a fine commander. You have a firm grasp of this war situation, and as all the cadres know, you are highly committed. I am very proud to have served with you on this very special assignment.

SOLDIER TWO [*a little embarrassed*]: Listen, you don't have to . . .

SOLDIER ONE: Honestly, I am proud to work with you. When this war is over, I am going to tell my children, and my grandchildren what a fine man you are. And to think I misunderstood you all this time.

SOLDIER TWO: Okay . . . that's fine. Let us talk about something else.

SOLDIER ONE: And you got so much modesty too . . . so self-effacing one would never guess the depth of your commitment, and of your great wisdom.

SOLDIER TWO [*beginning to lose patience*]: Please, I don't want to listen to this.

SOLDIER ONE: You are a man of few words, that's why. You are a man of action. Not like some of these cadres who revel in boasting about their experiences in prison. You just sit there and look indifferent whilst they go on about their past sufferings and the troubles they have seen. No, sir, you don't talk. You act. You go out on a mission and do the job.

SOLDIER TWO [*very angry*]: Will you shut up dammit!

[*There is silence as the men glare at each other,* SOLDIER ONE *is rather perplexed at* SOLDIER TWO'*s sudden outburst.*]

You don't ever want to stop talking nonsense, do you? I am sick of you, you know that? Sick! Sick! Sick!

SOLDIER ONE: Hey, what did I do now?

SOLDIER TWO: What did you do? What did you do?

SOLDIER ONE [*still puzzled*]: All I said was . . . I mean, I only said nice things about you.

SOLDIER TWO: I don't want you to say nice things about me. I don't want anyone to say nice things about me. [*Shouting hysterically*] I don't deserve it, do you hear that? I don't deserve the praise that you, and your bladdy Commander, and everyone else is showering me with! Can't you people leave me alone? Can't you let me fight this war in peace?

SOLDIER ONE: Okay, you are touchy about your good work, but for Heaven's sake you don't have to blow your top about it.

SOLDIER TWO: Touchy? Good work? God! Aren't you naïve! I am not the man you think I am.

SOLDIER ONE: Oh yes you are. Everybody knows that. Ask any of the cadres.

SOLDIER TWO: Listen, let's leave things as they are, okay? Let's leave this subject once and for all.

SOLDIER ONE: I am your friend, and all I want is that you should know that I admire you.

SOLDIER TWO: Stop saying that!

SOLDIER ONE: Honest I do. I know there is something troubling you, and I want you to tell me about it.

SOLDIER TWO [*trying very hard to contain his temper*]: Listen, pally, I don't want you to think I don't appreciate what you are trying to do. But I want to be left alone. I want to sort myself out, and I don't need your help to do it.

SOLDIER ONE: It must be what they did to you. I can see it all now. Reliving the past is painful because of all the dirty things they did to you in their torture chambers.

SOLDIER TWO [*taken aback*]: What?

SOLDIER ONE: That's it! I know you have told me you have never been inside their interrogation centres, but I know you are just saying that because you don't want to think about it any more. It's got painful memories. Or maybe you are too modest about it. It helps to talk about things, you know?

SOLDIER TWO: Who are you, man – some kind of psychiatrist or what?

SOLDIER ONE: Just a friend who wants to help. I understand the pain you have gone through, and I want you to know that I am with you. You know what? They are going to pay for all the things they have done to us. We are going to make them pay.

SOLDIER TWO: I wish you'd listen to me.

SOLDIER ONE: I got it! You are on a mission of vengeance. That accounts for all your bravery. They did all the dirty things to you in their torture chambers, so now you are out to get them. That's it! You have no time for words, for the past, because all you want now is to get even. I should have thought of that!

SOLDIER TWO [*sighs in resignation*]: I fell in love.

SOLDIER ONE: So you did, eh?

SOLDIER TWO: That's why I joined this war, because I fell in love.

SOLDIER ONE: Well, that's very nice, but it doesn't make any sense to me. I mean, people don't go about fighting wars just because they fell in love.

SOLDIER TWO: You'll be surprised to know how much that happens. Anyway it's a long story, and I don't want to bore you with it . . .

SOLDIER ONE: I am ready to listen.

SOLDIER TWO: Please, not now. Let's wait for the sign, do our work, and get out of here. Then maybe I'll tell you.

[*There is silence. The two men seem to retreat into their thoughts.*]

[*Sudden outburst*] She was a lovely woman! Very lovely! I loved her.

SOLDIER ONE *looks at him in amazement.*

SOLDIER TWO: I thought one day we would marry, have kids, you know . . . and live happily ever after.

[*He pulls* SOLDIER ONE *violently by the collar of his tunic.*]

Happily ever after, do you hear that? Like in the story books.

SOLDIER ONE [*freeing himself*]: All right, be calm, pally. Everything will be fine, I tell you.

SOLDIER TWO: She had no right to do that to me.

[*At this time one of our dark figures on the second level enters. She is dressed like the mourners we have previously seen and her features are just as indistinguishable. The hazy light of the past.* SOLDIER TWO *sees and addresses her.*]

You had no right!

WOMAN: I had no choice.

SOLDIER TWO: You had me!

WOMAN: But you had nothing.

SOLDIER TWO: I had everything. I had you.

WOMAN: I wanted more than that.

SOLDIER TWO *slowly and painfully walks to the second level.*

SOLDIER TWO: I still cannot understand what brought about this change. When we played together at the township playground, and the night fell on our games of hide-and-seek, it was enough that you had me. Other children looked for us everywhere, but would never find us, for our hiding place was deeper than they could understand.

[*He kneels before her and holds her hands.*]

We hid in each other . . .

WOMAN: That was yesterday. Today we have a different story to tell.

SOLDIER TWO: Until the angry voices of our parents screamed at us to come home. And both of us took the punishment from them for practising what was reserved for adults only: love. But we insisted until they learnt to accept the fact that we too were capable of loving. And we grew, and we loved. Oh, how we loved!

WOMAN: Yes, there was a lot of beauty those days. But it is not beauty that we eat.

SOLDIER TWO: I am going to be known one of these days. And my poems shall be read far and wide. Then I'll be able to give you everything you want.

WOMAN: In the meantime, while you slave in their factories and dig their quarries, what life is there for us?

SOLDIER TWO: Somehow we shall survive. Like all our people, we have always survived.

WOMAN: I have survived long enough. Now I want to live. Live, in the day and in the night.

SOLDIER TWO: We have each other.

WOMAN: And in the evenings, when others go out to dinners, and to theatres, and to concerts, we shall sit in our shelter and listen to obituaries on the radio.

SOLDIER TWO: Isn't that what families do? Obituaries are one of the most popular prime time radio programmes. Families sit around the portable and listen to them every week. I cannot change a tradition.

WOMAN: I have tasted better ways of spending my time.

SOLDIER TWO: But your ways cost money.

WOMAN: That is exactly what I am saying. It is no fault of mine, nor yours. I am glad that at last you see it my way.

A wedding song can be heard off stage.

SOLDIER TWO [*pleadingly*]: Please, listen to me. A new work ethic, they said. They are going to teach us a new work ethic at the factory. An ethic that will eliminate the greed that seems to dominate our lives. We can both attend the classes and life will be more meaningful for us.

Enter a man, followed by a train of revellers singing wedding songs. Their costumes contradict their gaiety, for they are all dressed like (and, in fact, are) the mourners we have met in

129

a previous scene. The man ceremoniously stretches his arms towards the woman.

MAN: 'Come with me, and be my love'.

WOMAN [*giggling, and holding his hands*]: That's cute.

MAN: It's from a poem of the Romantic era.

WOMAN: Tell me the rest of it.

MAN: I forget the other lines. I only remember, 'Come live with me and be my love'.

SOLDIER TWO [*laughs*]: And this is the man you want to leave me for.

MAN: I thought you would appreciate it, since I am told you write poetry of sorts.

SOLDIER TWO: I write poetry of this era. [*To woman*] You mean this is the man?

WOMAN: He has a Mercedes Benz.

MAN: And a fish and chips shop.

WOMAN: And a petrol filling station.

MAN: And a fleet of taxi cabs.

SOLDIER TWO *is dumbfounded. The wedding train, led by the man and the woman, sings and dances around him whilst he beats the ground with his fists in frustration. They go out.* SOLDIER ONE, *who has been observing the scene all the time, goes down to the second level, lifts* SOLDIER TWO *up, and together they walk back to the highest level. There are tears in* SOLDIER TWO'*s eyes.*

SOLDIER TWO: You didn't see them.

SOLDIER ONE: What?

SOLDIER TWO: The tears.

SOLDIER ONE [*looking the other way*]: What tears?

SOLDIER TWO *smiles, as they put their arms on each other's shoulders. Lights down on both second and highest levels, and*

130

rise on the lowest level as MAMA *and* NANA *enter.* NANA *is carelessly dragging her rag doll.*

NANA [*excitedly*]: At last we have arrived! Isn't the capital beautiful, Mama? Look at all those tall buildings, and the wide streets, and the cars, and the people, and . . .

MAMA: Yes, it is beautiful. We built it all, do you know that? It is our hands that built it.

NANA [*incredulously*]: We did?

MAMA: Oh yes, we built it. But we are not allowed to stay here, you know? Only they can live here, in all this glitter. All we do is build, and go back to live in the squatter camps.

NANA [*whispering*]: They must not hear you say that, Mama. They will lock you up.

MAMA: It is our life, child.

NANA: Where do we start looking for my papa?

MAMA: It is late now. We shall start looking tomorrow.

NANA: Where are we going to sleep?

MAMA: We must find a place somewhere. We cannot afford to stay in the places where you pay to sleep. And we do not know anyone here.

NANA: Maybe if we go to the township someone is going to welcome us into her house.

MAMA: Nana, people of the city are not like us at the squatter camp. Oh, with us a visitor is always welcome in our makeshift shelters, and to share our piece of bread with us. People of the city don't do things that way.

NANA: We have to sleep somewhere.

MAMA [*a bright idea strikes her*]: I know where we are going to sleep! You remember where we took our last rest . . . just before we entered this city?

131

NANA: Yes. That's the place where we saw those fenced-in buildings guarded by soldiers.

MAMA: That's right. Past the fenced area I saw a path that leads to the hill overlooking the soldier's place. The way I saw it, it's a bushy place . . . you know, trees and bushes. I am sure we can find a place to sleep there.

NANA: You mean we are going to sleep under the trees?

MAMA: We have been sleeping under trees and rocks throughout our journey.

NANA: But we are in the capital now, Mama. I thought things would be different.

MAMA: They will be different when we find your papa.

NANA: Isn't it dangerous to sleep out like that? I heard that the capital is crawling with hoodlums and robbers and all kinds of nasty people at night. They might rob or kill us.

MAMA: Don't worry child, we'll be safe. Why do you think I choose that place, and not the pavement or the waiting room at the bus stop? It's because those are places where you find crooks and robbers. What robber will risk going to a place which is infested with armed soldiers? So you see, we are going to be safe, child.

They go out. Lights fade to black.

Scene Two

It is late afternoon on the highest level.

SOLDIER ONE: You must have loved her . . . I mean, to join a whole war just because she married someone else.

SOLDIER TWO: That was not the reason.

SOLDIER ONE: You didn't love her then?

SOLDIER TWO: On yes, I did. But that was not the reason I joined the war.

SOLDIER ONE: You don't have to be ashamed of it, pally. It shows in spite of everything you are a very sensitive man. You wanted to forget. Or maybe you felt you didn't have anyone to live for any more.

SOLDIER TWO: No, not to forget. But to atone.

SOLDIER ONE: Man, I don't want to tell you a lie, and pretend that I am smart enough to understand you. A woman leaves you, so you join the war because you want to atone?

SOLDIER TWO: The sign! Where the hell is the damn sign?

SOLDIER ONE: Patience. That's one of the things you taught me.

SOLDIER TWO: You know what? I think I am done with this war. I think this is my last assignment. I am not cut out for this kind of work.

SOLDIER ONE: You are the last person to say that. Why, you have had more successes in all the missions you have been to than all of us . . . or at least most of us.

SOLDIER TWO: After this I am just going to walk back home.

SOLDIER ONE: Why would you want to do a thing like that?

SOLDIER TWO: Because I think I have accomplished what I came to do.

SOLDIER ONE: You don't think that would be selling out the rest of us? They know who you are, you know? They are going to arrest you, torture you until you reveal all you know about our movements. Then they are going to hang you. Man, even if you are strong enough not to reveal our plans, they are going to sentence you to die anyway.

SOLDIER TWO: Yeah, you are right. I am confused, man. I got to sort myself out somehow.

[*Once more there is silence.* SOLDIER TWO *is pensive, while* SOLDIER ONE *is both puzzled and worried.*]

[*Suddenly*] You know, in this country it is the easiest thing to take vengeance on your enemies?

SOLDIER ONE: Yeah, you shoot them.

SOLDIER TWO: No. You let the system do it for you.

On the second level enter our secret police (formerly Interrogators) as we have seen them before. They file in line, marching to an anthem, and stand to attention in a military fashion, facing the highest level. The hazy lighting of the past.

POLICE ONE: You called us?

SOLDIER TWO: Yes, I am the one who called you.

POLICE TWO: Come down, and let us hear what you have to tell us.

SOLDIER TWO [*scared*]: Actually, it was a mistake. I didn't mean to call you. I mean . . . I have nothing to tell you.

POLICE THREE: He is afraid.

POLICE ONE: Don't be afraid. We shall not harm you. Come down here and let us talk.

POLICE FOUR: You haven't broken any law, have you?

POLICE THREE: Of course he hasn't broken any law. Would he have called us if he had broken the law? He has something very important to tell us. But he is very afraid. [*Cajolingly*] You come down now, and for sure we are going to protect you.

SOLDIER TWO *gives his gun to* SOLDIER ONE, *and starts to walk down to the second level.*

SOLDIER ONE: No! You can't go there!

SOLDIER TWO: I have to go. I called them.

He goes down. POLICE THREE *meets him halfway. He holds his hand reassuringly, and gingerly walks down with him to the second level.*

POLICE THREE: We are the keepers of law and order, and protectors of helpless citizens.

POLICE FOUR [*threatening*]: You'd better have something to sing about.

POLICE THREE: Hush! He called us, didn't he?

POLICE ONE: I am sure he has news of law and order to sing about.

SOLDIER TWO: It's about a man.

POLICE [*repeating after him*]: It's about a man!

SOLDIER TWO: He owns a fish and chips shop.

POLICE: Fish and chips shop!

POLICE THREE: But that's not a crime.

SOLDIER TWO: Wait till you hear.

POLICE FOUR: Come on, sing faster.

POLICE THREE: Hush, the song promises to be interesting.

SOLDIER TWO: And a fleet of taxicabs.

POLICE: Taxicabs!

SOLDIER TWO: He drives a Mercedes Benz.

SOLDIER ONE: We know who you are talking about. We have our finger on everything.

POLICE MAN: Yeah, that's the man who was getting married last week.

POLICE FOUR: Did you call us to tell us that a man is doing well in his business?

SOLDIER TWO: There is more to it than that.

POLICE: More!

SOLDIER TWO: Well, as you said, you have your fingers on everything. Maybe you know all about it already, eh? You must let him go on the way he does so that you can catch more of his comrades. I know you are very smart fellas. I am sorry I wasted your time.

POLICE FOUR: What comrades?

POLICE THREE: His comrades, silly. Don't you worry, man. You haven't wasted our time. As a matter of fact we are proud of citizens like you. We are going to give you a commendation.

SOLDIER TWO: No, please, not a commendation!

POLICE THREE: Okay, we won't give you a commendation. But I would like you to know that what you are doing is very honourable. Now, tell us all you know about the man.

SOLDIER TWO: I was at the wedding. I know the man through his wife. So I overheard everything. The man has connections with the guerrillas . . . I mean, the terrorists. Apparently he has been making large donations to their war effort. Some of the profits from his business go out to finance acts of sabotage against our beloved fatherland.

POLICE ONE: This is the greatest song we have heard in a long time.

POLICE TWO: We never could have suspected him.

POLICE FOUR: Speak for yourself. I suspect every one of these people.

POLICE THREE: But the whole thing doesn't seem to make sense. Why would a budding capitalist want to support a communist-inspired war against the very law and order that protects his own interests?

POLICE FOUR: You never know with these people. I don't think they themselves know what they want.

SOLDIER TWO: I heard it with my own ears, sir. They didn't know I was listening. There was a man who came from the guerilla camps. I saw him, sir, and I heard that he had come to collect the money. She knows about it too ... I mean his wife. She is involved in the whole business too. You go and ask them, sir, then you'll know that I have told you nothing but the truth.

POLICE THREE: We want to thank you for your most beautiful song.

SOLDIER TWO: There is more too, sir.

POLICE: More!

SOLDIER TWO: He has been recruiting young men and women to join the war against the state. He has been using his trucks to smuggle people into the training camps. His wife knows all about it too, sir.

POLICE THREE: We need more men like you. There is hope yet. I am telling you, with men like you this country is going to know peace. You will be rewarded for this – immediately after giving evidence in court against the man and his wife.

SOLDIER TWO [*scared*]: Evidence? I thought we agreed that no one will ever know that I sang.

POLICE THREE: Don't you worry. You will stand in the witness box as Mr X, and your face will be covered with a mask. Your identity is safe with us.

They march out to the anthem. Lights rise on the second level, and from now on all the levels belong to the same space and time. SOLDIER TWO *attempts to climb back to the highest level.*

SOLDIER ONE [*pointing the gun at him*]: You stop right there!

SOLDIER TWO *stops.*

SOLDIER ONE: I am not giving you your gun back. In fact I am not letting you come near me. I want to hear the rest of this sordid affair first. I want you to tell me why you sold this man out, and put our whole war effort in jeopardy.

SOLDIER TWO: I didn't put the war effort in jeopardy. The man was not involved in anything.

SOLDIER ONE: So you lied about him because he stole your woman.

SOLDIER TWO: I was bitter against them both, for treating me the way they did. I was completely blinded by my own frustrations.

SOLDIER ONE: What happened to them?

SOLDIER TWO: She is there . . . in the township . . . running the businesses.

SOLDIER ONE: And the man?

SOLDIER TWO: You know, I feel better now that I have told somebody.

SOLDIER ONE: What happened to the man?

SOLDIER TWO: He died, damn you! They took him to their torture chambers and demanded a full confession.

SOLDIER ONE: But he could not sing because he knew nothing.

SOLDIER TWO: He was not used to torture. He was soft and flabby, so he died in the torture chambers. The interrogators made a statement that he died of a heart attack in one of their offices while they were having tea and discussing terrorism. You are the first one I have told this story, and I feel relieved. Now you can shoot me if you want to.

SOLDIER ONE: You want me to shoot you?

SOLDIER TWO: Go ahead! Shoot me!

SOLDIER ONE: I find it difficult to figure this out. You think you know somebody, only to find that all this time you have been deceiving yourself. Perhaps people were never meant to be known . . . to be understood. I cannot trust you with me here, especially now that I am the only one who knows your secret. You might try to kill me or something like that.

SOLDIER TWO: I give you my word.

SOLDIER ONE: Why should I take the word of a traitor?

SOLDIER TWO: I have proved myself, haven't I? Long before you joined this war I proved myself. You yourself have been blabbing about my commitment to this war. Don't you think I have atoned?

SOLDIER ONE: An innocent man died in their hands.

SOLDIER TWO: In return I have mined some of the most dangerous places right inside enemy territory. I have sabotaged railway lines, and blown up power stations. How much can a man pay?

SOLDIER ONE: And you think that mitigates what you did?

SOLDIER TWO: It does not, but I think I have atoned for it.

SOLDIER ONE: Man, I am confused. What am I going to do?

SOLDIER TWO: Give me back my gun.

SOLDIER ONE: And what next?

SOLDIER TWO: Then we shall await the sign. You know that to accomplish this mission there's got to be two of us here. There is no other way out.

SOLDIER ONE: You know of course that when we get back I am going to tell the Commander about you – if I'll still be alive?

SOLDIER TWO: You'll still be alive, trust me. I am going to do my damndest to see to it that this mission succeeds. And after that we are both going to join the cadres – alive. Have no fear about that.

SOLDIER ONE: And you know you might be put on trial? Even if they don't execute you, no one will ever trust you again.

SOLDIER TWO: I want my last mission to be a triumph, whatever fate awaits me.

SOLDIER ONE *throws the gun at him. He catches it and starts to move up.*

SOLDIER ONE: I think I am a fool.

SOLDIER TWO: You won't regret it.

SOLDIER ONE [*trying very hard to convince himself*]: Maybe your atonement was enough. But I am no judge of these matters. It is the cadres who will decide.

SOLDIER TWO *extends his hand to shake* SOLDIER ONE'S.

SOLDIER ONE: No, I cannot shake your hand. Our relationship shall be purely business. I don't want to be your friend any more.

SOLDIER TWO: That's what I had asked for even from the beginning of our wait. But no, you would have none of that. You wanted to be friends. You wanted to talk and tell me of your sufferings.

[SOLDIER ONE *walks out.*]

Where are you going?

SOLDIER ONE [*off stage*]: I want to take a walk. Got to think about this.

SOLDIER TWO: Don't go too far now, or you'll expose yourself to the enemy. Also remember the sign might come any time, and we got to be ready for action when that happens.

On the lowest level enter MAMA *and* NANA.

NANA: This might be the right place.

MAMA [*pointing to the second level*]: Let's try up there. It looks more comfortable.

They climb slowly to the second level.

MAMA: This is the place.

NANA: I am so tired I want to sleep right away, Mama. Right after feeding my baby.

They sit down, and are about to prepare to sleep when SOLDIER TWO *sees them, and points his gun at them.*

SOLDIER TWO: Who is there?

NANA [*screaming*]: Mama, it's a bandit! He has a gun!

SOLDIER TWO: Come up here with your hands up.

MAMA: Please do not shoot us, my child. I am a poor old woman with a little girl. We do not have any money.

MAMA *and* NANA *go to the highest level.*

SOLDIER TWO: What are you doing here?

NANA: He is going to kill us, Mama.

MAMA: We came to sleep here.

SOLDIER TWO: You don't have a house?

MAMA: We are strangers in these parts, my child. We come from the squatter camps many many miles from here. It took us days to reach the capital.

SOLDIER TWO: Sit down. I'll see what I have in my knapsack for you to eat.

141

He opens his knapsack and takes out some dried fruit. He gives it to them, and they eat.

NANA: He is a nice bandit, Mama.

MAMA: Are you a highway robber, young man?

SOLDIER TWO: I am not a robber. You shouldn't be here, you know? It's very dangerous.

MAMA: What are you, if you are not a bandit? Surely you are not a soldier. You look different from the soldiers we saw when we came here.

SOLDIER TWO: I have no time to answer those questions. I want you to go away from here. Finish your food and go away. I don't want my comrade to find you here. He might not be as nice to you as I am.

MAMA: So you *are* a bandit then.

NANA: I told you, Mama, this place is not safe. We should have gone to ask for a place to sleep in the township.

SOLDIER TWO: Don't worry, little girl, no harm will come to you. At least not from me.

SOLDIER ONE *enters, and is amazed to see* MAMA *and* NANA.

SOLDIER ONE: Mama! Nana! How did you come here?

MAMA: Nana, tell me I am dreaming.

SOLDIER TWO: You know each other then?

NANA: It is papa!

SOLDIER ONE: How did you find me?

MAMA: What are you doing here?

NANA: I was right, Mama. He is not in prison. We walked for nothing. He deserted us to be a bandit.

MAMA: I wouldn't have believed it if someone told me that my own son is a gun-toting highway robber.

SOLDIER TWO: He is not a highway robber.

142

SOLDIER ONE: We are not bandits, Mama. We are soldiers. I left home to join the guerrilla army.

MAMA: You should have told us. We walked all this way because we thought you were suffering in prison.

SOLDIER TWO: You don't announce to the world when you join the army.

SOLDIER ONE: He is right, Mama. It might leak out and the secret police will know all about it.

SOLDIER TWO: Listen man, I am going to leave you with your family for a while. I am sure you have a lot to talk about. But don't be long now. You know we have a job to do.

He goes to the second level and lingers for some time. He has a very pained look.

NANA: I am very sorry I believed those who said you had run away, papa.

SOLDIER ONE *kisses her.*

SOLDIER ONE: Listen, you must go away now. And don't tell a soul you saw us here. Go back home and help the people to rebuild.

NANA: I am not going back home, papa. I am staying here with you.

MAMA: You know you can't stay here, Nana. We've got to go back home.

NANA: But I want to be a soldier too, Mama.

[SOLDIER TWO *has overheard this, and we can see that a bright idea has struck him. He laughs aloud and raises his fist in a gesture of triumph. The others look at him in amazement. He goes out. A gunshot offstage.* SOLDIER ONE *runs to the second level and goes out.*]

The soldiers are attacking, Mama!

SOLDIER ONE *comes back and, as if dazed, walks back to the highest level.*

SOLDIER ONE: He did it. It's all over.

MAMA: What is all over?

SOLDIER ONE: Everything. The assignment. He killed himself, Mama. He shot himself dead.

NANA: Why?

SOLDIER ONE: It's a long story. There is no time to explain. He was a brave man, Mama, and he shot himself. No, it's not all over, Mama. I am going to complete this assignment. I cannot do it alone . . .

NANA: I am going to stay with you, papa.

MAMA: You cannot do that, Nana. You are only a child. I am going to stay.

SOLDIER ONE: I am sure that's why he was not afraid to kill himself. He knew that the mission would still be accomplished.

NANA: I am not going back home alone. I am the one who's going to stay. Papa can teach me what to do when the sign comes and I'll do it. I am a soldier too, and I am going to stay here with him.

SOLDIER ONE: She has made her case, Mama. Let her stay.

NANA: Take my doll with you. I'll get it when I come back home. I hope it won't die whilst I am away.

SOLDIER ONE: Mama, you better go away right now. We don't know when the sign will come.

MAMA: I find it difficult to leave.

SOLDIER ONE: Mama, your stubbornness will not only put our lives in danger, but the lives of hundreds of cadres.

[MAMA *reluctantly takes her small parcels and walks to the second level.*]

Tell them to keep the home fires burning. We are coming.

NANA *takes the gun, and sits next to* SOLDIER ONE. *Lighting gradually changes and the two soldiers become silhouettes of statues in some war memorial. When* MAMA *gets to the second level, she is joined by the mourners, now holding candles. A plaintive voice leads them in a song whilst they hum in the background. They slowly lead* MAMA *to the lowest level and all go out. Lighting fades to black.*